Becoming A Fly Fisher

DEDICATION

To my wife, Mary, who has made all of this possible, and to my children and grandsons, the family and the future.

BECOMING A FLY FISHER

From Brookie Days to the Tenth Level

By John Randolph

The Lyons Press
Guilford, Connecticut
An imprint of The Globe Pequot Press

The Lyons Press is an imprint of The Globe Pequot Press.

Printed in the United States of America

Designed by Compset, Inc.

10 9 8 7 6 5 4 3 2 1

Library of Congress Cataloging-in-Publication Data is available on file.

Contents

Introduction

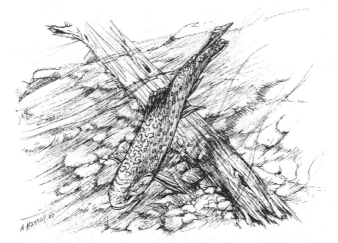

The Main Stem

For five decades I was mesmerized with learning the libretto of fly fishing, and then I paused to listen to its music and heard the measure between its notes. I had fallen into that trap described by Edward Ringwood Hewitt: First an angler thirsts to catch fish, then to catch a pile, and finally to catch the largest one of all. Unfortunately, the revered fly fisher and author forgot to add the final, most important, stage: just being there . . . listening, seeing . . . better yet, observing. Better yet, reaching that mature melding of knowledge and perceptions that creates metaphor. He should have mentioned that we follow side channels as fly-fishing technicians in search of magic potions.

We rush hopefully along the trail—discovering a magic fly here, an enchanted rod there, a line that adds fifteen feet to our cast. We become technically proficient, and old, before we become wise.

This book is written for the young, on whom much will be wasted but for whom all is new, and possible . . . and ahead. For, as novelist Tom McGuane noted: "Angling is where the child, if not the infant, gets to go on living." And the child can live with extended passion for a very long time. He can go on learning, and thrilling, and loving . . . if he doesn't lose his way.

I worry that this generation (X, or Y, or is it Z?) has such shame about leisurely recreation that it has no ability to just be still or, as Vince Marinaro once advised, to sit and play a "game of nods." I worry when I see would-be fly fishers carrying digital counters, as though the catch-per-hour is the equivalent of an uptick (or downtick) on a stock tape. The fly fisher who carries a cell phone onstream commits a sin, both to himself and to the sport he pursues. He may never become a fly fisher, for the communicable disease that grows in his heart is purpose, the psychological steroid of ambition. His fraternal numbers are growing, and if they reach critical mass, our sport may not survive with the spirit and values that we inherited from our high priests of fly fishing.

Introduction

———

This book will trace our original spiritual heritage. It will describe the religion of fly fishing, for that is what our sport is, and uniquely so. And it will search for those inspiring values embodied in special fly fishers who have fished the Main Stem—as close to Heaven as we get here on earth.

We are always in a state of becoming in our search for the eternal natural truths that make fly fishing a sport apart. We may never enter the fly fisher's Tenth Level, but it is the journey in search of it that is spiritually fulfilling. Fly fishers have historically comprised a special brotherhood (and, recently, a sisterhood). A contemporary comedienne had it right when she observed: "We are all in this together ... alone." Or as a young Maryland fly fisher informed his mother recently: "Fly fishers are different from other people, Mom. We're not like you."

I will write about fly fishing's special values, its sacred beliefs. I will describe what turns some fishermen into fly fishers. This is not a Vade mecum or an epistle; it is a psychological epigenesis in which the fishing boy becomes the fly-fishing man. Of necessity I must trace my own genesis, for in the nature-nurture game I'm all I have to work with. I understand my own peculiar *Umwelten*, how my cultural perceptions (inherited, absorbed, and taught) formed values that opened the doors of fly fishing to me and created *my world*.

Becoming a Fly Fisher

—

x

HUNTERS OF FISH

Barry Lopez says in *Arctic Dreams* that the evidence is strong that among all northern European aboriginal hunting cultures, the hunter saw himself as bound in a sacred relationship with the larger animals he hunted. A similar relationship with fish enriches the soul of a fly fisher.

Lopez explains the aboriginal hunting relationship this way: "Hunting in my experience—and by hunting I simply mean being out on the land—is a state of mind. All of one's faculties are brought to bear in an effort to become fully incorporated into the landscape. It is more than listening for animals or watching for hoof prints or a shift in the weather. It is more than an analysis of what one *senses*. To hunt means to have the land like clothing. To engage in a wordless dialogue with it, one so absorbing that you cease to talk with your human companion. It means to release yourself from rational images of what something means and to be concerned only that it 'is.' And then to recognize that things exist only insofar as they can be related to other things." (A fly fisher would insert the word *water* for *land*.)

Lopez says that the dreaming mind is a nonrational, nonlinear comprehension of events in which slips in time and space are normal. He compares it to the conscious working mind of the aboriginal hunter. Also, the focus of a hunter in a hunting society is not killing animals but "attending to the myriad relationships he understood bound him into the world he occupied with them. He tended to those duties carefully because he perceived in them everything he understood about survival." A fly fisher would nod in understanding.

Then Lopez describes how modern man has separated himself from his natural world: "A fundamental difference between our culture and Eskimo culture, which can be felt even today in certain situations, is that we irrevocably separated ourselves from the world that animals occupy. We have turned all animals and elements of the natural world into objects. We manipulate them to serve the complicated ends of our destiny." A fly fisher would nod again in understanding and agreement.

Fly fishers try to reconnect themselves to the natural world the way the aboriginal hunter is connected to his world. The fly fisher of yesteryear and today senses a hole in his soul created by the coldly objective, impersonal values of his modern culture. Onstream he seeks to reconnect with the animals (fish) that he pursues. And he seeks to connect with them personally. He does this by first learning the intimate secrets of his home stream—its geography, its hydrology, its aquatic insect biota, its moods. He seeks to learn its fish, and particularly those fish that are the eldest members of the population. When he has become adept enough at catching them, he releases them because he wants, once he has made physical contact, to continue his magical, personal connection with a wild living thing in the future. And he is afraid to be alone again, back in the swirl of everyday life, cut off from the magic that has made him feel whole, perhaps for the first time in his life.

The fly fisher feels, in those preternatural moments, "an extravagant pleasure in being alive." He may also feel an almost ethereal escape from his confining intellect into the magical world of the mystic. He may even experience the passionate embrace of something outside himself, a release from estrangement and despair, a reconnection with an archaic feeling for the land and the water. He may discover that "profoundly secret pass that leads from fate to freedom."

As usual, Thoreau may have said it best in *Walden*:

I found in myself, and still find, an instinct toward a higher, or as it is named, spiritual life, as do most men, and another toward a primitive rank and savage one, and I reverence them both. I love the wild not less than the good. The wildness and adventure that are in fishing still recommend it to me. I like sometimes to take rank hold on life

Introduction

---

and spend my day more as the animals do. Perhaps I have owed to this employment and to hunting, when quite young, my closest acquaintance with Nature.

These are complicated cause-and-effect relationships that, in the end, have much to do with what we call the heart, or what Native Americans describe as their religious animus, a feeling that a spiritual landscape lies beneath the physical one, and that it is only at certain little-understood, mystical moments that it is revealed. Sometimes, deep in a river, the fly fisher finds that the stream itself is like poetry, coherent, transcendent, and with the power to elevate the meaning of human life.

These fleeting moments of heightened physical intensity—the sound of mayfly wings in an evening hush, the sight of broad trout noses hog-wallowing along a weed line, the flash of bonefish dorsals on a sunlit flat—lead us to believe that there is another realm of reality coincident with the real one, but different. Fly fishers seek to find it, to reconnect with it by being out there where it can happen . . . again . . . and again. How often have we heard that old refrain: "Boy, if I was retired I'd be out here every day after the big kahunas!" We realize that the great totemic fish are *good to think*. They are the objects of our devotions. They are *good to imagine*.

Partially glimpsed, these images spur our imagination and we fill in the rest. We glimpse a riseform on flat water, a snout, and we imagine the heavy body underneath, the hook-jawed mouth, the vermillion-colored gill covers. When we glimpse effervescent bubbles on glassy water in a quiet lagoon on the Amazon, our imagination creates the good-to-think twenty-pound female peacock bass underneath that is guarding her young and that will savagely attack our fly when it is cast into the school. When we spot bunker being driven wildly up against the beach by marauding striped bass, we inhale the smell of pickles on the salt air and dash down the beach to cast into the wild melee. The image of a fifty-pounder slashing at bait in those waves drives us.

How often have we stood in a stream or on a flat and sensed the coming—when we felt natural elements combine to reveal the numen, when the curtain separating real and spiritual parted and we glimpsed the inner life of a stream or a flat? We search longingly for those physical margins where it will happen again, and we demand that our professional guides *make it happen*. There are certain places where we know to look. They are the edges of our landscapes—a bend in a river, the seams between back eddies and main currents, the flats along the mangrove islands, the riptides where the tidal flats drain to the sea. They are the margins between *what is* and *what is becoming.*

These are the fly fisher's twilight places, where things happen between fish and their food. It is in these places that we, the hunters, expect to meet them and fulfill our expectations. Our mind map creates our expectations; we know that the fish will be in certain places, whether it is on our favorite stream, a cut, or along a barrier island where the tide washes a point. Our experience in these places fills them with memories: "The Dutchman's Hole," where I hooked Old Henry and he ran me down into the logs and broke me off; Sands Cutt, where I hooked that double-digit bone and got cleaned by a coral stub; Barnhardt's, where Jimmy rose the big brown to his Hendrickson spinner and the fish broke 4X. A fly fisher's mind map is a congerie of such places, and his map enlarges with the years as he wanders the world in search of fish and the Zen that surrounds their meetings with men and flies.

This book will describe the drives that impel us to hunt fish with flies. It will also describe the spiritual joys and aesthetic fulfillments that fly fishers find so captivating and compelling. And it will describe the secret pass to the watery mansions we would enter and the doors and channels that lead to them. When we are ready to say, "It is time to be old and wade the shallows," we will talk of mysteries. Then we will tell our grandchildren: "The mystery is Nature herself; now go and find her."

In the summer of 1997 I had arranged to fish the idyllic Bourne in Hampshire, England with my guide, William, on a bright June day near the village of Hurstbourne Priors. William parked the car and we strode leisurely down through flowering fields toward a line of trees that marked the small chalkstream made famous by Harry Plunkett-Greene in his delightful book *Where the Bright Waters Meet.* As we walked, William gave a brief biography of the concert opera singer, who from 1902 to 1912 lived in a house beside the road where we had parked the car. As we neared the stream, William led me into a weedy country graveyard and stood beside a small headstone.

"This is where Plunkett-Greene chose to be buried, as close to his beloved Bourne as he could manage," William said reverentially. With that he retrieved a clear plastic box from his fishing jacket, knelt, and placed it carefully on the base of the grave. In

Introduction

—

the box was an Iron Blue Dun, Plunkett-Greene's favorite fly for the Bourne, tied by William in the knowledge that we would fish the Plunkett-Greene water that day. The tiny box took its place with others placed there by Plunkett-Greene admirers.

We left the graveyard and its cathedral hush and walked silently to the Bourne. I fished its clear, skinny waters and hooked and lost a large trout in the grotto of trees below the bridge downstream of the viaduct pictured on page 68 of Greene's book. Although the Bourne is a pale shadow of its glory years at the turn of the last century, I felt the presence of Plunkett-Greene as I fished. And as much as any author who has enriched the literature of our sport, he represents the wisdom that the fly fisher finishes his life with but one river.

This book is about the Plunkett-Greenes of the world and those who have followed them. My hope is that the boy from Maryland, and others who share his passion, will continue along the less trodden path of the fly fisher. Their reward will be to sit on the bank of the perfect trout stream whose quiet enameled surface is broken only by dimples and dark heads. Memories of a thousand waters will stream to them, and they will sit and savor the deliciously immodest sucking sounds of feeding trout. They will not then, after long years of hunting,

Becoming a Fly Fisher

—

be moved to cast a fly or yell "Yeehaw, I hooked another one!" for all to hear. Sitting there, alone, they may choose just to watch. They will have reached the Main Stem, where they will feel no urge to hurry.

> I give you the end of a golden string,
>> Only wind it into a ball:
> It will lead you in at
>> Heaven's gate. . . .
>> John Donne

—*John D. Randolph, October 15, 2001*

Acknowledgments

There are many fly fishers who have reached the Tenth Level of fly fishing, and who became regional fishing legends during my lifetime. To them I owe an enduring gratitude for the values and skills that they have taught me, in person or through their writings. In Pennsylvania they include Jim Leisenring (*The Art of Tying the Wet Fly*, 1941), Charles Wetzel (*Practical Fly Fishing*, 1943), Vince Marinaro (*A Modern Dry-Fly Code*, 1950, and *In the Ring of the Rise*, 1976), Dr. Alvin Grove (*The Lure and Lore of Fly Fishing*, 1951), my friends Charlie Fox (*This Wonderful World of Trout*, 1963, and *Rising Trout*, 1967), Ed Koch (*Fishing the Midge*, 1972), Ed Shenk, George Harvey (*Memories, Patterns and Tactics*, 1998), and Charlie Meck (*Meeting and Fishing the Hatches*, 1977, and other books).

I learned techniques and disciplines from West Coast steelheaders and trout fishers Enos Bradner, Roderick Haig-Brown (*A River Never Sleeps*, 1946, and other books), Trey Combs (*Steelhead Fly Fishing and Flies*, 1971, and *Steelhead*, 1998), Don Green, and Les Eichorn of the Sage Rod Company. Other great steelheaders

Becoming a Fly Fisher

—

influenced my learning, including: Jim Pray, Claude Kreider, Clark Van Fleet, Tommy Brayshaw, Al Knudson, and Steve Raymond (*The Year of the Angler*, 1973, and *Steelhead Country*, 1991). Russell Chatham (*The Angler's Coast*, 1976) through his writings taught me fishing style and commitment. I learned about nymphs, after years of frustration, from Polly Rosborough (*Tying and Fishing the Fuzzy Nymphs*, 1965). My good friend and fishing partner Jim Teeny taught me how to catch Pacific salmon and winter steelhead. My soul brother Mel Krieger (*The Essence of Fly Casting*, 1987) taught me the spirit of fly casting, and the Rajeffs, Steve and Tim, showed me how it can be done at the championship level. I owe much to Dan Blanton, Hal Janssen, Lance and Randall Kaufmann (*Bonefishing with a Fly*, 1992, and *Bonefishing*, 2000), who taught me to see more than fish on the flats of the world. I owe Mike Michelak and Bob Marriott, men who demonstrated that great fly shops are the spawning and rearing grounds of our sport. Andy Puyans, by example, created in a generation of San Francisco Bay Area youth, and in me, the love of tying flies to match the hatch. I learned about fly lines from Myron Gregory, and through the writings of Larry Green, I slowly came to understand the lore of West Coast fly fishing. Walton and Pres Powell helped me understand its spirit.

Acknowledgments

———

xxi

In the East my teachers included, either in print, by influence, or in person: Theodore Gordon (*The Complete Fly Fisherman*, notes and letters of Gordon by John McDonald, 1947), Ray Bergman (*Trout*, 1938), Lee Wulff (*Atlantic Salmon*, 1983), Edward R. Hewitt (*Hewitt's Handbook of Fly Fishing*, 1933), Colonel Joseph D. Bates (*Atlantic Salmon Flies and Fishing*, 1970), Roy Steenrod, Rube Cross, A. J. McClane (*The Practical Fly Fisherman*, 1953), Herman Christian, Walt and Winnie Dette, Harry and Elsie Darbee (*Catskill Flytier*, 1977), Larry Solomon and Eric Leiser (*The Caddis and the Angler*, 1977), Ernest G. Schwiebert Jr. (*Matching the Hatch*, 1955, *Nymphs*, 1973, and other books), Art Flick (*The Streamside Guide to Naturals and Their Imitations*, 1947), and Ellis Newman. I especially want to thank Leon Chandler, who led the Cortland Line and Twine Company for fifty years, introduced American fly fishing to Japan, and taught the fly-fishing industry the rules of gentle behavior. Thanks to Tom Rosenbauer of the Orvis Company (*Reading Trout Streams*, 1988), who explains fishing in understandable text, and Al Caucci and Bob Nastasi (*Hatches*, 1975), who taught me the importance of reading what is in the stream and under its rocks. And my thanks to Art Lee, who, with Galen Mercer, kept the Catskill tradition of dry-fly excellence alive and well.

Becoming a Fly Fisher

——

My instructions on upper Midwest trout and steelhead came, indirectly, from pioneers Art Winnie, Leonard Halladay, Paul Young, William Blades (*Fishing Flies and Fly Tying*, 1950), Doug Swisher and Carl Richards (*Selective Trout*, 1971, and other books), Robert Traver (*Trout Madness*, 1979, *Trout Magic*, 1983, and other books), Gary Borger (*Nymphing*, 1979, and *Naturals*, 1980) and Bruce Richards, the Scientific Anglers line engineer and master caster and angler. And thanks to Kelly Galloup (*Cripples and Spinners*, 2001), who teaches us how to catch steelhead and trout in new ways.

In the Rockies I owe my instruction to Charlie Brooks (*Nymph Fishing for Larger Trout*, 1976), Dan Bailey, Fred Arbona (*Mayflies, the Angler and the Trout*, 1980), Tom Morgan, Phil Wright, Mike Lawson, Rene and Bonnie Harrop, Al Troth, Bud Lilly, George Grant, Gray LaFontaine (*Caddisflies*, 1981, and other books), George Anderson, Paul Schullery (the classic *American Fly Fishing*, 1987), Bill Klyn, Jack Dennis, Paul Brunn, Craig Mathews, Phil Gonzalez, George Kelley, John Bailey, Ross Marigold, Craig Fellin, Dave Decker, and Bob Jacklin. They have been mentors to generations of fly fishers from the East and West, and to me.

In the South the great innovator and friend to our sport Dave Whitlock (*Guide to Aquatic Trout Foods*, 1982) created revolu-

Acknowledgments

---

tionary fly patterns designed to catch bass and trout on the White River in Arkansas. Slowly his influence spread nationwide, and he became the master in hair and feathers as well as instructor to the world in fish behavior, angling techniques, and the joys to be found through fly fishing.

Working from his home in Maryland our friend Lefty Kreh (*Practical Fishing Knots*, 1972, with Mark Sosin, *Fly Fishing in Salt Water*, 1974, and other books) became teacher, father figure, and mentor to the entire world of fly fishing. His presence and his writings have changed us for the better, whether we are learning to cast or attempting to solve the riddles of fly tying and fishing. In England my friend John Goddard (*The Trout and the Fly*, with Brian Clarke, 1981) taught me how trout see and react to the dry fly. The Great Bear, Hugh Falkus (*Sea Trout*, 1962, and *Salmon Fishing*, 1984), taught fly fishers how to see trout and salmon as ethologists see them—behaviorally. And my thanks go to Nick Lyons, with whom I worked for many years in editing and publishing *Fly Fisherman* magazine. To Nick I owe my love and understanding of fly-fishing literature and its great influence on our sport.

These men, and others, through their instructions and their writings, opened doors for me into fly fishing's spiritual fulfillments. It is to them and to my family that I owe the gift of happiness.

Chapter One

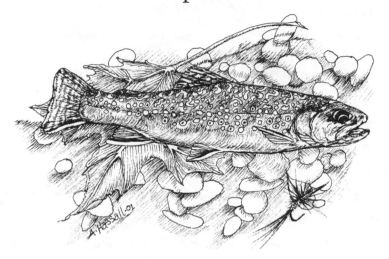

Brookie Water

When I was a boy I lived near a stream that held small brook trout. It was a perfect brook for a small boy. And now that I am a man I realize that much of what I have observed in my life of fishing has been shaped by water and the things living in and around it. My values are drenched, aqueous, water-driven. That brook in a pasture in the Berkshire Hills began and shaped it all; my experiences in my home brook annealed my soul to water and its music.

I like water in streams. It moves and makes noises that express its pleasure, impatience, and anger. It plays high up in the places where the brook begins. Up there, where the ferns grow around the rivulets and runnels, it tinkles and makes small hollow roars when it plunges into pockets that smell of frog and trout. It's nice to lie on the cool banks in such places and watch for furtive shapes. The water there runs white over moss. My first trout I laid on that moss, and the speckled sides, the water, the green, and the lilt of musical water sounds have not left me.

The water falls always and all ways. It slides and sheets across ledges. It tumbles over boulders and fans lazily across amber- and gold-colored sands. If the brook tries to trap the water, it will not be held tightly. It shoots down waterfalls and runs white with impatience. In the woods it runs very dark, as if the light of life had gone out of it. There, its delicious dampness grown somber, it seems to need time to be by itself, away from sunlight and our view. The brook trout there are reclusive, too; their backs ripple the surface of pools glimpsed far ahead. The fish are scared of everything, even themselves. Where they dart, they send scary little water Vs up and down the surface. There is no reason for them to be so edgy, but they always have been so, and always will be. Mortal terror is in them.

Brookie Water

————

Then the brook emerges into a promising sunlit pasture. The water idly meanders. It slides into corners and piles up against a raft of drift from a recent freshet. Fish noses appear and disappear in the soft eddy line that weeps away from the pile.

Water like this calls for a quick flick of the fly, but I cannot resist reclining on the bank to watch the leisurely feeding. Golden bubbles float on a burnished surface gilded by sunlight. A soft whirring in the liquid air draws my attention upward. A shimmering ball of backlit airy effervescence dances above the stream, lowering, then rising and lowering again. A mayfly lands on my ear. I let it stay, content to be just a resting place for an ephemeral creature near that meeting place of mayflies and fish.

As the swarm of flies falls to the water, the fish quicken their feeding. They are famished, wild things abandoning fear for brief food. Their rises become quick and urgent, and soft sucking sounds echo from the pool.

From where I sit, I cast my fly to the fish with a slight sidearm flick of the wrist. It lands like thistledown and quickly disappears in a whorl of water, and for the first time I feel something live in the rod. At my feet the trout looks angry and surprised, as if this disturbance in its feeding is not yet perceived as life-threatening.

In the net it wriggles when softly grasped. Its eye becomes globular and alarmingly large, all-seeing and terrified. Its flanks are silky with a lustrous sleekness. Out of its element, it shines with an iridescence that will disappear quickly like rainbow light if I kill it. Held briefly with its chin in the water, it shoots away, a waterborne sliver of energy captured and then released.

Each winter, when the pasture was locked in sheet ice and our sled runners made that running sound down through the orchard, we waited. Everyone waited. The first hopeful signs came on the lengthening afternoons of March when, following the snow patches uphill through the icefields so we could stay upright, we spotted the first under-ice rivulet. Lying on our stomachs, we could watch the mercurylike silver bubbles form and hear them gurgle beneath the ice where the tiny springlets pushed upward toward the sunlight. The pastures were unlocking, and the little brook running in its clean, dark, and somnolent cleft through a dazzling white snowfield would soon shake itself and roar.

In late winter the brook bubbled up here and there from the ground as springs along the pasture hills. In spring we tiptoed along the spongy ground and the earth bubbled around us. When it rained, the organic smell of the earth's bowels lay on the land. The clouds, which had scudded cold and tight across

Brookie Water

———

November hills, now were light-shot and floated like pillows of white cream with tinges of raspberry. When cloudbursts sheeted down, the sheep paths bled white and the pasture's quartz out-croppings shone very white and clean where the green grasses spread a new carpet under the white birches.

Then, while tiptoeing along the quaking ground where the springs rose, you could spot a hole in the sod with a clear rivulet pushing up like new hope. If you bent down over the hole, you could look into the eye of the earth itself. There, mini sand parti-cles danced as though buoyed by the essence of the bleeding ground. The water seemed to be a pure and secret liquid. It would be revealed to us only for a week or two, and then the bubbling springlets retreated again to their dark, safe underworld.

We knew that the spring season was special for the waters, so we turned out and walked the land and watched those places where in the past the secret springs had revealed themselves.

There were other springs, too. The large ones established little cauldrons for themselves, intimate little grottos, each with a bright green frog to leap and cloud the pool when we knelt to drink, and always on a hillside where the earth on a humid August day was cool and damp and all fern smell. It beckoned to us to stop a while and dip our hands into bone-chilling water and sift the pool free of leaves and watch the spurts of water jet thinly up through the tenebrous liquid until the spring, miraculously, cleared. Then we would search for the porcelain cup left there for passersby. We would take one of those long, deep drinks. We always lingered there before heading off through the hot pasture, and the springs were, and still are, the oases of our dog days.

These were the springs that oozed and spurted and trickled their way down to form the little brook where the brookies waited to brighten the days of little boys.

When the brook had quieted after the flood, it became quite interesting to children who, in their innocence, had decided that the fields and streams were Mother West Wind, the Leatherstocking Tales, and Jack London on the Chilcoot Trail all rolled into one. During that brief and delightful idyll, this brook was my teacher, my friend, my succor, and my great hope for Leviathan conquest.

How intriguing were its intimate places. Where it trickled out of its tiny headwater swamp, it meandered in a narrow slot winding through dark sod banks. When you approached near, with rod in hand, the throaty sound of the brook running within its confinement made the hair raise on the back of your neck. Within those private little recesses, you know, finned, unglimpsed except in the imagination, the Leviathan of all brookies.

Brookie Water

It didn't take long to discover that there were trout in every teacupful of water. And my partners in sport soon learned how much the little things loved worms dangled into their frothy pockets. You could draw a crowd of hungover adults out of bed with a mess of those beauties lying cleaned and all damp and shiny on a bed of ferns. But we soon learned that catching them by hand under the stream bank earned the highest praise for woodsmanship.

We practiced the technique on that little slot of water. It was so small that you could crawl up to it on your knees and lie on your belly with the grass warm on your stomach and your shirt-sleeves rolled up and the smell of trouty brook water in your nose. If you stuck your arm down over the bank slowly into the icy water, it would scare the brookie into its hiding place under the bank. Then you slowly felt each nook and cranny in the cold bouldery recesses of the hole until you touched something soft. You grabbed and lifted your arm and all at once threw the flipping trout back onto the bank at someone's feet and yelled "There!"

Downstream the brook ran in against a bank with an undershot ledge. It was good for two trophies each time you drifted worms through. It was uncanny how the brookies replaced themselves in that little hole, and we always wondered if we'd fished it out. But there was always a grand competition for the worm as it drifted and wriggled into the lair. The brook was the absolutely perfect brookie place, and it could outproduce any boys with hooks and worms and hands. Since then, acid snow and rain have done what the boys could not. The brook has so few trout that I do not fish it anymore. Each trout killed would be an assassination, perhaps of an entire race. Then it was a feast; now it is a memory.

So the little brook slides openly down into the giant oaks and you expect to take two trout there—and you do. But all the while you are anticipating something, as though hoarding a special cookie to devour last. The waterfall pool is ahead.

You hear the waterfall first, a shimmering sound like aspen leaves showering on a tree in an autumn breeze. It raises goose bumps on your forearms. You stop and kneel and check your worm box. A plump, pink-purple one will do the trick. You pluck the soggy gray thing off the hook and discard it and bait up, ever so carefully burying the hook point in the firmest flesh near the head. Ready.

The approach is woodscraft of Indian-like beauty. Slithering along on your stomach to the old apple tree at the head of the ledge flume, a long white ribbon sheeting across black rock, you peek one eye around the trunk at its base. There!

Oh what a trout! The Leviathan of Workman's Brook! And looking, too! He's up on his fins and watching like a linebacker awaiting the snap—intent, fixed gaze, fins waving, holding in the current just below the plunge water. He's at least eight inches long!

You sneak your rod around the tree until the tip is just above the water chute and then drop the tip and reach the line and worm bouncing down into the white boil. The trout shoots forward as though hit by an electric shock and grabs and you lift. The brook spits its shimmering rocket into the sheltering tree branches. You leap at the flopping tree ornament and grasp cool, live flesh and fall to the ground hugging it. But even then, with all its exultation, catching and killing a trout was no small tragedy, and so it remains for me today.

Important things happened in that pasture. And the brook ran through and trout lived in it and made the boys happy on days when all the world was summery. I think of that place always, though other streams and other fish have taken their places in my book of angling days.

RIVERS

Sometime along that little Berkshire brook I eased into the idea that moving waters have their own animus. They live. This has become for me a semi-religious belief. And because I believe, I am a fly fisher.

For a long time brooks and rivers were, for me, just places to catch fish, the larger the better. And there was so much in the fields and forests that was catchable that my attention seldom focused long on the little hillside streams. Had I lived by a great chalkstream where great trout show themselves, my understanding of rivers and streams as living things might have flourished. I might have come quickly to my love of them for themselves. But though I arrived late, I reached waywardly the mecca to which some anglers travel.

Streams and rivers, a fisherman believes, are the arteries and veins of the earth. We hunt for fish and the search brings us to the moving waters. Inevitably it is the beauty of those places that we recall. The trout and the rivers are inseparable, bound together. And when the trout vanish, the boot tracks on the sand soon disappear.

I have searched, poking into this river valley and along that meadow, wandering—free. And I cannot say which compelled me most, the spiritual beauty of the places where trout and salmon live or the spirit of the trout themselves and the delicate, mutable hatches on which they feed. Perhaps it doesn't matter.

During those moments of exploration, time is suspended. Then, in the quiet places where trout rise freely, for a few moments I am connected, and momentarily immortal.

Along the journey, I began to make natural observations and connections whose explanations I found only in the writings of Thoreau and John Muir. The idea of plant, mineral, and animal sentience, so common among the primitive cultures of the world, grew slowly in me. I began to realize that in my moments outdoors, alone, I discovered, as Muir says, that "every hidden cell is throbbing with music and life, every fiber thrilling like harp strings, while incense is ever flowing from the balsam bells and leaves."

Fly fishers know this. We explore and fish the great rivers of the world. We discover when we search out *Ephemera*, and trace their beginnings to the stream bottom, that they are connected to everything else in the universe and we begin to feel that a heart like our own must be beating in every nymph and dun.

The trout, the hatches, and the rivers bring us together across all geographic boundaries and social differences. The wealthiest *estancia* owner in the foothills of the Andes discusses flies with a truck driver from Brooklyn. On no other social playing field can they meet as equals. The only status a president of the United

States has on a great fly-fishing stream is what he earns there—through his fishing. He is welcomed as a bird of feather.

Fly fishers define rivers in strange ways. A freestoner is a fast-moving, rocky stream that tumbles down a mountainside in impetuous leaps and turns, dashing through runs and tumbling into frothy white pools. It has a rocky bottom, and it tends to spate great flashes of freshet water when rain sheets down.

Freestoners are where we begin our fishing. They are easy. The trout that live in them are hungry, for food is scarce. A boy can take his worm jar and wander from pool to pool, fishing his way up to the hard-to-reach special spots near the headwaters. With a little experience on his own, he learns that somewhere up there is a mossy ledge that weeps cold, clear water. It's the birthplace of the stream, a special wellspring that he husbands in his memory against hard times.

Freestoners are easy to approach stealthily. The trout lie in the shelving pools ahead, facing upstream and into the current, on the lookout for that rare drifting morsel of food—a blackfly larva dislodged from the underwater rocks, a worm washed down from a stream bank. The trout must strike quickly or the food will be swept downstream and lost in an instant. If he misses too often, he will starve. He's a sucker for a fly or a worm.

Freestoners are exciting places. And once a boy has learned their secrets, he moves on, discovering himself as he explores the water. He learns that virtually any dark fly floated on its pools brings a splashy rise. He also discovers that the trout will not take the fly if it drags. On the mountain by himself he experiments with line and fly, and he improves. Slowly he becomes a drag-free fisherman who appreciates the sight of a trout taking a fly on the surface. He grows; he is ready to try a fly of his own making. His rewards are self-taught and hard-won.

As he matures he discovers the rare nature of large fish in small places. Subliminally he senses that large trout surviving in small, lean places *are the animus*. He catches and learns from small fish, and he begins to work his way downstream to the richer water, where the big fish lie. He discovers that any break in the flow can conceal a trout. And he learns that a beaver pond can create the place where little trout become fat. He begins to haunt streams where the beavers live, and the trout he brings home are the stuff of rumor.

He is followed to his secret places by friends. When the trout quickly disappear, he becomes secretive. His spots are woods pools of magical bounty. They can be defiled by intruders. The rare spots must be protected. He becomes a conservationist: The trout have become so important to him that he declines to kill them. For the rest of his life he will carry that ethic with him.

Good streams, he decides, are alive, rare, frail, ephemeral, pure, and honest. They are spiritual places, rich select envelopes of aquatic glory that diffuse evenly throughout his entire being. In these places his feelings of spiritual vacuity and enervation disappear. In these places the ancient differences between the animate and inanimate dissolve into a living harmony.

He works his way downstream, fishing a nymph or a streamer ahead. He learns how to keep a tight line so as not to miss the quick jerk and rejection of the fly. And as he fishes the broader, slower valley water, he notices that the stream has changed in other ways. It has become a small river, with broad, deep pools and chutes, slicks and tailouts. He has never encountered such waters before, and he discovers that the river animus has changed, too. His casts are to rising trout, fish that take their time and inspect their food. The trout are often larger than the quick mountain fish, but they are also more so-phisticated, for they have been fished over repeatedly there where the roads are near and the fishermen many. The river has large hatches of mayflies, caddis, and stoneflies, insects that are strange to him.

He meets another, older, fly fisher and he inquires into the nature of the "bugs." There in the stream he receives a crash course in stream entomology and his mouth drops. A whole new world of challenges and knowledge has opened to him. He will never be the same person, an innocent. Bigger trout have turned him downstream. The paradigm of the perfect trout streams with ideal hatches compels him to wander the streams of the world.

Fly fishers believe that spring creeks have special importance. They rise in clear upwellings from deep in the earth's recesses. We assume, because we can see the clear evidence, that they are especially pure and untouched by the poisons of human creation. Their waters are cold enough for trout but not too cold for insects. They are a natural, lucky, conspiracy of good things happening in small, beautiful places. To fly fishers they are like quiet semi-religious grottos where one can pause to be alone.

Spring creeks are so rare that their reputations call to us, and we whisper of them in the faint hope that they will remain secret. The first sight of one can be an epiphany to a young fisherman. Suddenly, in flat, clear water, there is a large fish feeding languidly on the surface, and on tiny mayflies! He watches the fish in absolute awe and abject fear. The fear of failure overwhelms him. His hands tremble. He cannot recall the sequence of things that should be done. He decides to sit and watch and plan his approach and the correct presentation of the fly.

It should be from below. Yes, that's right. The trout is feeding comfortably. He can ease into the water just below the fish and cast the fly up and over it. The drift should take the fly directly down to the trout.

He checks his fly box for a Pale Morning Dun imitation. His hands tremble and he spills the little box of flies at his feet. He retrieves them and hurriedly refills the box and, glancing nervously to see if the fish is still there, ties the tiny fly on. Then, unsure of the knot, he reties it and pulls hard to check the connection. The thin tippet snaps with a *ping*. He reties the knot and straightens the tippet material carefully again and again until it remains straight.

The trout rhythmically picks floating duns from the edge of a swirl. It supports itself in the surface by planing its pectorals and waving its tail. Its large snout lifts and then falls, then lifts again. The water spilling over its head and shoulders is humped.

Mayflies slide to the left and right of the hump, unmolested. The snout lifts again gently and an insect disappears.

He has seen enough. It must be done now. He edges down the flat bank to a spot fifty feet below the fish and tiptoes into the water. He tosses line to and fro into the air until he estimates it is enough to reach the target. He tosses and the line end hits beside the snout. The fish disappears.

Despite his considerable skill, he will fail to catch the spring-creek trout. Year after year he will fall short, haunting the waters, observing the habits of large, old fish, presenting his fly unsuccessfully. In these places he feels closer to the animus than he has ever felt before, though the little mountain streams continue to call him back for doses of success and rejuvenation. The spring creek, he senses, is a mature living place. Water and plants and trout move languidly. The fish seem to understand and value their importance, feeding with the restraint and judgment of epicures. His hunting instincts concentrate. They must. Failure provides him with a sustained frustration fed by adrenaline.

He searches for answers from stream veterans and from books. And the reading and questioning make him a communicant with the elders, the wise men who have written of their successes and failures. He discovers the literature of fly fishing, the instructional and the inspirational. It dawns on him, slowly, that he is not unique, not especially sagacious or artful. Others have followed the same streams, with similar dreams, long before him. They have encountered the same challenges, opened the same doors, tied the same flies, made identical presentations, suffered the same defeats.

It also dawns on him that his journey toward some dimly perceived fly-fishing nirvana will be endless, a trip through an expanding fish envelope. He will travel, change, improve, develop. But he will never actually become. He might attain Level Nine, but Level Ten, the spiritual and actual plane of perfection, will never be his. He slowly realizes, from his reading, that it is the journey that is important. The journey itself may *be* Level Ten.

The mind has a way of sketching important memories in raised relief on a matte gray background. Failures join the fisherman's dead pool of dreams—of great fish encountered and, somehow, lost. They signify something but he cannot perceive what it is. Nor can he understand why, in midpursuit of idols, the quest for perfect fish is so strangely obsessive-compulsive. It is as if he lives life on two planes, the first the endless trail of life's dreary obligations and commitments and the second his fly-fishing obsession. *Kill the boy in the man and you kill the man* he repeats to himself as his justification for his trips to quiet waters where the soft whir of mayfly wings and the sipping of trout punctuate the silence.

He discovers that the long-term memory is kind. He recalls that evening on a river in England when the pursuit reached Tenth Level, and he *knew*. He witnessed his own birth there, almost as an out-of-body experience, when it began to happen, when the river's slumbering spirit stirred to send the mayflies up and to bring the trout to the surface to meet them around him, when they, surprisingly, included him, without prejudice, in their celebration. It happened, though, after he had acquired his skill, after he had learned how to take and release the fish. Perhaps the trout and the river *knew* and allowed him to take.

He started slowly that day. The river's keeper had instructed emphatically, "The fishing must be upstream dry fly, sir, and only to rising fish." He had swallowed hard. No searching with nymph or streamer when the water was riseless?

He plopped down on a wooden streamside bench and sat dejectedly watching the glassy water of the Test slide down channels of ranunculus and suck loudly through weed-clogged carrier gates. It was weed-cutting day on the river, a half-price day for the paying angler and a nymph-filled day for the trout, which fed happily beneath the slick surface. He daydreamed. Something caught his attention near the water's edge. A water vole paddled busily by and then climbed ashore and sat on its haunches and nibbled a tendril of weed. It was so *Wind in the Willow*–like. He daydreamed chapter 2, then 3 and 4, trying to recall the detail of each character and personality. The river slept.

When the sun set around eight-thirty, a single fish dimpled the surface way upriver and he rose stiffly to investigate. As he approached the willow where he had seen the dimple, he noticed a certain nervousness in the water's surface near the bank, as if the velvety coverlet of the river held something live and excited underneath.

He knelt beside the stream and, with his eye low to the water, looked upstream into the surface glare as though sighting along a rifle barrel. In the pewter-colored sheet glare he could see tiny dimples. The water bulged and rippled nervously. Trout! Feeding trout! Large feeding trout! Gluttonous trout! They made a thousandfold sucking sounds, the smacking of many tiny lips in the delicious twilight.

Brookie Water

His hands quivered in the darkness as he attempted to tie on a small dry fly while clenching the tiny flashlight in his mouth and turning away from the stream to shield the light from the fish.

When he had the fly on, he cast up and to the right of the urgently feeding pod of large trout. They were intent, preoccupied in gluttony. It was happening. The secret magic of the earth's veins and arteries was revealing itself here, now, and perhaps nowhere else in the world at this instant. He was a witness and, perhaps for one special moment, a participant.

His casts snaked out to the right distance, paused in the air above and to the right of the fish, and then retreated. He let the next cast go, directly above the feeding lane this time. The fly settled and he saw in the surface sheen the telltale plip where it landed.

He could not see the fly then, but he judged where it must be—just downstream of the little dent it had left in the water— and when another plip appeared in the bulgy surface, he lifted his rod and felt a live, electric throb.

The trout rushed from the thin bank water into midstream and he played it there hurriedly until he could grasp its cool slipperiness and release the hook from its mouth. He knelt again, quietly searching the glare above him where the other trout still fed as though unconcerned with what had happened behind them.

He presented the fly again and took another fish and then another. He wanted to make it last forever, that moment of acceptance. He caught large trout there for a long time in the darkness. Then a hooked fish splashed amid the feeding throng and the door to Level Ten slammed shut. The river was silent, introverted again.

Chapter Two

Hatches

That evening on the Test I had to wait twelve hours for a chironomid hatch to set the table for the trout. It was worth the wait, for it is the hatches and where we find and observe them as trout foods that color our values as fishermen. They lead us to truths about our fishing, about the behavior of fish, and more. When we encounter a hatch and immerse ourselves in matching it, life blazes forth with unnatural clarity and we suddenly possess new senses. When we are young our instincts are to catch and kill, but our experience teaches us to observe, to be quiet, to catch, and, finally, to be gentle.

As a boy I had no shame. I chummed fish with live grasshoppers before offering the one with the hook. Slowly my values grew and I developed into a fly fisher who can control his urge to catch. Today I would not stoop so low to conquer . . . but who knows, given an encounter with that one true Leviathan, what my price has become? My hands quiver at the thought of a great hatch of large mayflies and the large trout that rise to them. The mayfly duns and the large trout are *my candy*.

There were no hatches to see on Workman's Brook. So the worm was my way until I finally fished downstream to bigger water, to the Green River. The first hatch I can recall clearly may have been Hendricksons. A fishing partner and I had come to the Green in May to fish, and as we leaned over the railings on the old iron bridge to spot trout and suckers in the blue-green water below, a disturbance in the tailout of the long pool caught our attention.

Trout dimpled the surface here and there, and lightly floating insects drifted with wings tucked high like little sails. As we watched, we saw that the dimples always came where the mayflies were, and, upon closer examination, we noticed that the flies disappeared with the dimples. The trout were feed-ing . . . *on them.*

No two boys ever got their worms into action faster. Or took less. Or departed with more hangdog looks and excuses. We sim-ply could not understand how trout could feed and dismiss worms. They never had before.

Once the river became our haunt, mayflies became the bane of our trout existence, until one day an outsider appeared and began taking trout—on the surface! He flicked something deli-cate on a fine line and rod and let it ride along for a while until a trout tipped to the surface and made a ring. Then he lifted. And the trout was on! And he caught so many fish—as many as he wanted, it seemed to us. His creeled sagged heavily at his side.

We asked him how he was catching those fish. He said he was fly fishing. He showed us his flies and they looked like the bugs we'd seen in the air. It all became clear then, clear that we knew nothing and might never know anything in a world of arcane adult lore. We trudged off and fished our worms and thought about it. We caught very few fish.

All would have remained hopeless for us except that about that time my father and his pals discovered fly fishing and in-cluded us. We were old enough to swim and thus could risk the big river, where the mayflies and the big trout lived. My father and his friends taught us how to cast the line and to present the fly upstream so the moving water took it back to us without drag.

They explained the hatches, too, but we could make little sense of it, except that bugs hatch in water and trout eat them. They said something about "matching the hatch" and gave us some flies with which to do it, but the best I could manage was to watch the water, pluck a floating fly from it, and match it with something from my small box of flies. Usually the trout were on something else. My fishing was frustrating and often without hope.

But then there were those magical days. They usually happened in May about the time the apple trees and shadbush blossomed and the cows were freshly turned out to pasture. It was a good time to be young and in a place where all living things were in a warm and green renewal.

Especially the mayflies. We soon learned that May was their special month on our river. It was a freestone river, with a bouldery bottom and fast runs of white water followed by long glassy pools. It seemed so fresh and optimistic in spring, when the freshet waters filled it and made it roar. During those chilly days we fished it respectfully from shore with bright streamers. The fisheries people stocked it for the opening day, and the hatchery rainbows were foolish and hungry and caught the fly at the end of its swing. We laid them in proud ranks of twelve-inchers on the bracken ferns. After admiring the catch, we loaded our baskets for the trudge homeward up Workman's Brook.

Gradually the river became calm and wadable, and then the air above it filled with dancing insects that, for a brief month or two, brought the trout to the surface to feed. During those days, the cedar waxwings took up residence there and perched expectantly on the streamside branches, awaiting the midday hatches. To be onstream during the meetings of mayflies, waxwings, trout, and fishermen was a feast of anticipation and fulfillment. As the May sun sent its soft lever of light down into the Green River valley, the mayflies popped to the surface. The trout were waiting and indulged themselves sucking down the flies. The waxwings left their perches and wheeled and pirouetted above the water, snatching mayflies from midair, and we joined in the feeding festival. We were there when the river shared her most intimate secrets. We were marked, imprinted with the fly fisher's special love of moving water and dancing mayflies and sipping trout.

In summer the little river lost its confidence. Its flow dropped slowly, the boulders revealed themselves like some great river skeleton, and the waters became good for swimming. The mayflies disappeared then and the trout vanished into the depths of the big pools or ran up the cool mountain brooks. We followed them. The Green River, you see, was a poor place for mayflies. It would be years before I understood why. It would be decades before I fully comprehended the good fortune of boys who dwell near the great mayfly rivers of the world.

The great mayfly places spawn great dry-fly fishermen. The insubstantial hatches of the Green created an incompetent dry-fly youth. The Pennsylvania streams, with their great hatches rising from spring to autumn, set the table for the trout each day, and the young Marinaros, Foxes, Leisenrings, Becks, and Harveys who haunt their banks soon learn that the trout will be up and on the take predictably. Great mayfly rivers also create great fly tiers—Gordon, the Darbees, and the Dettes on the Beaverkill; Skues, Halford, Clarke, and Goddard on the English chalkstreams; Swisher and Richards on the Muskegon.

When I finally reached the little Green, I discovered the big trout, none larger than two pounds, but to me a two-pounder was a giant. I discovered them first with worms and spinners, but quickly the pure fun of catching rising trout on drys changed me: I became a voyeur of hatches and trout.

Hatches

The idea slowly dawned on me that there was more to fly fishing than catching fish. To be successful one had to understand mayflies and other aquatic insects. Fly casting required hours of practice. Fly tying lay at the heart of successful imitation—of matching the hatch. One could not succeed on the water without an understanding of it.

There were fishing techniques to learn. How to present the imitations without drag; the art of nymphing; the disciplines of dry-fly fishing; and the effectiveness of streamers on large trout. There were books to read on how to do it, and they inevitably led me to the books explaining *why* we do it and thus into the fine writing of the only sport that has it own literature.

It was all mind-expanding, demanding, and overwhelming. How could one ever expect to achieve even the levels of the advanced amateur? My compulsion to catch more and larger fish on flies drove me on. Vastly ignorant of my lack of knowledge on fly fishing, but determined to prove that I could do it, I stayed with it. And in me there is proof of Twain's warning: "Don't part with your illusions. When they are gone, you may still exist, but you have ceased to live." I never parted with the belief that I could, in those special hours of relaxation and learning onstream, match the hatch, present the fly, and catch large trout.

There would be a career, a family, and all the responsibilities, re-wards, and dross of life, but because I started where I did, in that place, with a brook, and a river, and trout and mayflies, the boy became a man who fishes with a fly. The urgency of catching fish slowly recedes now, but the natural connections that surround the fishing are deliciously important, and the recollections of great hatches remain as fresh as spring rain. Hatches punctuate my book of angling days.

The days had been hot and then wet. Then the temperature along the Clark Fork of the Snake dropped suddenly to freezing. Gary LaFontaine said he knew of a place where the *Baetis* hatched at two in the afternoon on days such as this. We would be there waiting.

We parked by a great sweeping bend of the river and ducked under the interstate highway bridge for protection from the wind and blowing snow while we awaited the hatch. An occasional trout broke the surface.

"They're ready for it," Gary said. "What have you got in your box for *Baetis* imitations?"

Hatches

—

I picked through some beaten-up Adams patterns and held one up hopefully.

"Should do the trick," he said.

Half an hour later the fish were up and just under the surface, not holding in feeding lanes but dashing urgently here and there as though frantic for the next bite. They were beginning to roll. We'd given them time enough to fix on the hatch and, in their feeding frenzy, to ignore our presence.

We cast urgently, slapping the flies to the water six feet away at the base of the riprap where the giant back eddy of the pool turned back to meet the main flow. There the trout had queued to feed on the little hatching insects. They were coming to the surface fast now, and the trout burned it with their gluttony.

Their feeding infected us and we cast hard and fast, our faces flushed with the frenzy of man and fish and cold wind. The trout refused the little Adams at first, but when I clipped its hackle flush along the bottom, it suited them and we caught trout fast and released them hurriedly, knowing that the rise would end soon. We fished hard without talking; there was no time. And in an hour it was over and we collapsed on the bank momentarily and then climbed the bank toward the car and its warmth. That day has always seemed important, both in its promise and its fulfillment, and perhaps more so in its speechless companionship.

In eastern Oregon, near the town of Prineville, the Grindstone Ranch extends as far as the eye can see across the high desert. Lakes bulldozed into this moonscape grow trout the size of footballs. You fish them from float tubes paddled slowly, suspended in cool breathable latex. "Immersion technology" has made fishing comfortable in this nearly weightless world and, rocking gently in the icy morning air, snug in Polarfleece, you doze happily.

When there is no hatch on the water, the accepted tactic here is to kick gently, then stop. When you kick again, there will often be a nice tug on the line and you are hooked to the largest trout of your life. This is the Heaven of all heavens, an oasis in the desert where cold water combines with natural fertilizer to produce trout with jowls and heart conditions created by gluttony.

The night preceding this adventure had not been promising. Lance and Randall Kaufmann had lured me to the place with the promise of fishy sugarplums that would warm my soul. They did not mention that we would sleep in a deserted cinder-block ranchhouse where the pack rats had set up housekeeping.

In the twenty-degree inky blackness I lay in a sleeping bag stretched on a bedspring—listening. Small rodent feet scurried somewhere nearby, perhaps in another room where Randall lay—also listening . . . or in another where Lance slept.

"Lance! Lance!"

"What?"

"There's a rat in here! On my sleeping bag!"

"Go to sleep, Randall. It won't hurt you."

Skim ice lay like windowpanes in the puddles along the ranch road the next morning as three bleary-eyed pilgrims headed down to the lake and kicked off into wisps of mist.

Only an occasional dragonfly buzzed by that warm autumn day as we fished the small lakes gleaming like blue sapphires beneath mesquite hills. As the sun set, a chill gripped the lake, and when I dipped a hand beside my tube, the fifty-eight-degree water felt warm. A trout rose silently to my left and another to my right. Four mule deer stood silhouetted on the pallid skyline with ears pricked, listening.

A warm hum filled the air above the water. Size 14 *Chironomids* danced in the pale sky above my tube and dark trout backs broke the glassy lake surface. A fish splashed near Randall's black out-line by the earth dam, and he played it to his tube. A pack of coyotes yipped wildly in chorus somewhere along the ridge.

Trout fed to my left and right. Tails, heads, and dorsals sur-rounded me, rising and falling silently. Something bumped my leg. I was *in a hatch,* in that verging where the two worlds of in-sects and fish intersect.

I sat listening to the whirring and the gentle rises of large trout. My hand gripped my rod and did not move. I had no urge to fish.

The soft whirs of mayfly wings are the evening vespers that whis-per to us. Small mayflies, morning *Tricorythodes,* do not create the hum. Their tiny wings, moving in a mating swarm, sound like gases effervescing. But the larger species—sulfurs, brown drakes, and eastern *Ephoron*—emerge and fill the air with the softest mel-lifluous sound. To hear it is to sense delight through every pore, and sympathy with the fluttering wings makes us whisper.

One night I fished the White Fly hatch on the Susquehanna River near my home. I call it the "catfish hatch" because the flies emerge in such massive numbers that they entice these habitual bottom feeders to the surface to gulp. I can stand in the river when the *Ephoron* whir softly by the millions into the pale evening sky and observe a link connecting ephemeral life.

This emergence becomes impressive when the hatching multitude discovers that you are the only molting post available on the river. The irrepressible hatching insects must molt *somewhere*, either while flying, trailing their shucks, or on anything available. This night it happens to be me.

I stand there watching my waders and shirt gradually accumulate dozens, then hundreds, then thousands of naturals. They land, then each begins its transformation, shedding the skin that holds it captive as a dun. Then they fly away as spinners to land and drop their eggs. While I stand there I'm immersed in a multitudinous *insect instar*.

But that is not the entire experience on this sultry summer night when the river fills with the earthy smells of hatching mayflies and fish. Standing there when the hatch is in full swing, I hear the soft slurps of catfish that have swum up from the deeper water into the shallows to suck in the river's brief offering of insect candy.

They cruised in the surface, sucking five, ten, then dozens of naturals in a slurp. It would be my only shot at them this year, or any year, on a fly.

The tactic is to crouch low to spot the moving bulges their heads make as they cruise to and fro in the evening surface glare, sucking in floating flies and making a chorus of loud *slurps*. The reflected lights of Marysville help me spot the feeding cats. I must cast ahead of the fish so that it intercepts the fly. But which way is it moving? . . . left, no right, no ahead now!

I cast one length of line repeatedly so that in the darkness my sense of distant touch informs me instinctively where my fly has landed on the water. I will hook only one out of five presentations. Then there will be a surface explosion, a sudden toilet flush where the fish was. If it's a big one, it will break off 3X. Double-digit cats are out there sucking down mayflies. I'll need backing for this. It's the only time I'll need it on the river this summer.

I recall the Missouri's hatch sounds near Craig, Montana. One night, as the evening light faded under a cloudless sky, the caddis came in a massive upstream migration. The river sighed in the background and fish rose to the surface and sucked down the floating naturals. Then all the fish joined the feeding: The whitefish slurped; the brown trout sucked; the rainbows inhaled; and we lashed water splattered like birdshot with riseforms in desperate attempts to participate in the free-for-all.

It was not to be. There were simply too many naturals on the water—we could not compete. We stood listening: Nature had hiked her skirts, but we were simply voyeurs.

One evening last summer I fished a quiet pool on a stream near Cooke City, Montana, when the trout came up to feed. It was a special hour between sundown and darkness on a stream I had not fished since July 1957. The wind dropped and a hush fell across the valley. The water flowed gently where the current split around an island and eased into a bend hole.

I stood for an hour watching the surface of that pool, listening for the telltale *plup* of a trout. Only the murmur of the water and the haunting cackle of a sandhill crane broke the silence.

The trout slowly started to feed. A small, lazy ring appeared above me near the bank and slid downstream. Then another one appeared up and to my left. I stood waiting and watching—knowing what would come. It did, too. The trout settled in to feed on top. They got happy. I let them have their way for a while so I then could have mine.

I scooped a spentwing off the surface and held it in my hand. Its body—about Size 20—was a mahogany color; its wings were as clear as cellophane. I tied on a Rusty Spinner and began fishing to the nearest trout. It sipped. I lifted. It ran strongly downstream away from the feeding pod of fish. Five minutes later I held and examined a cuttbow and released it.

I had my way with them until dark—fishing the flavs.

I was stalking slowly up a small spring creek in western Montana, my eye fixed on the sparkling water ahead. I had spotted the stream's location by the cottonwoods that marked its course, and after chatting with the rancher who owned it, I'd been given permission to fish, provided that I closed all the gates on my way.

The ranch quarter horses lazed hipshot in the warm midday sun, and as I walked through the green meadow grasses toward the creek, grasshoppers chit-chit-chitted around me and the horses stirred and then ambled with me and nuzzled me for sugar.

Hatches

I had the whole day and the entire creek ahead of me. It would be a good day.

I stood and watched the little creek for a while, but nothing stirred except a muskrat nibbling something along the bank. A dry Montana wind sent waves along the tops of the shimmering broom grass. The langorous mood of the place took me and I began to drowse. I eased down on the bank in the sun and gave in to it. The clean washing sounds of the stream lulled me and my eyelids drooped. I dozed.

It was a deep aggressive rise. Nearby. Made by a very heavy fish. The *thuulush* of it sent me bolt upright. My eyes and hands and face, flushed with sleep, went suddenly cold. On the far bank, beside a trailing black alder branch, rings spread across the water's surface and the current took them slowly downstream into the small riffle below, where they disappeared.

I watched that alder for a long time. The little muskrat came and went; the horses nudged me again and departed, disappointed, and the breezes that had riffled the pasture grasses pushed their tops urgently.

Up the bank a way a grasshopper took flight. Its wings clicked as it flew and the wind swept it to the surface of the water. Its legs kicked and it turned giddily and foolishly as it tried, desperately, to swim toward the far bank where the alder trailed its limbs in dark, foreboding water. The hopper gained a little in its urgent efforts, but a current eddy caught it and sent it spinning and bobbing down along the alder limb.

When the trout came, it did not sip the insect; it shot up as though on tracks, propelled by a little cannon somewhere near the stream bottom. I had never witnessed such a commitment, so complete an abandonment of natural caution and survival instinct. The large trout, a survivor of five or six years in nature's snake pit, simply let it all go. It rocketed upward and grabbed, its momentum shooting it into the air in a kamikaze take.

I slapped a hopper pattern into the lie and quickly caught the eighteen-inch brown. It was a setup; how could I miss? But the truth revealed by that fish had changed me, as it would change anyone who casts a fly. I had observed one inner trout compulsion. The fish that consume so much of our attention are imperfect beings, feeding predators designed and compelled to eat the floating insects in the water envelope that is their world. But in that perpetual "I eat therefore I am" pursuit, marked by that shy and upward, vigilant stare in search of drifting edibles and enemies, they will always be suckers for a piece of candy. And we will offer it to them.

Chapter Three

Casting

Emerald green from the river to its top, the mountain shot up into a cobalt sky. Sheep as white as milk halted on tiered paths and stared down at us blankly. Across the river a mob of cheviots suddenly bolted then halted. The sheep stared back toward us as though we had exclaimed something of great import.

I felt like we would be watched while we fished. I decided to ignore them and get my gear together. There beneath the choirs of bleating sheep I withdrew a little 4-weight from its leather case to begin what has become an important ritual.

I ran my hands along the smooth graphite of the tip-top section and checked for nicks and examined the rod closely for scratches. I pointed it skyward and sighted along it. I examined the butt section and withdrew a small bar from my pocket and waxed the ferrule. I held the two sections up to the sky and aligned the guides by sighting down the rod. Then I pushed gently but with even pressure until the two pieces seated firmly.

The rod was light, but now it had a willowy life in it. I strung it with line and flicked it gently back and forth and the line and rod made a soft swishing sound in the air as I gradually stripped line from the reel and let it slip through my line hand and up the guides. The line took life in the air, snaking out, wavering. Then with my backstroke it withdrew cleanly, holding tight and almost alive, like a poised cobra's head.

The rod gained a life of its own, and I could feel the energy vibrate down from the tip to the ferrule and then, as the line sang softly out into the air, to the butt. I kept at it until I hit the wall at seventy-five feet and began to strain the cast and had to tell myself to relax—to think the stroke.

I wanted to light that brief intimate bonfire of sensual delight known only to the distance fly caster, the home-run hitter, and other superathletes—the light that warms your arm when you shoot a ninety-foot cast with a two-inch loop from a 5-weight rod.

Casting

—

43

I pumped the backcast high and fast and stopped the rod hard with a tight squeeze to allow the tip to accelerate. Before stroking forward, I followed through, reaching back and up to allow the line to straighten fully. Then, with my left hand, I reached up the line toward the stripping guide as I brought the rod forward in a slow acceleration to straighten the line. I gave an instantaneous stroke and pull, stopped the rod hard, and popped the tip back.

The line formed a tiny loop off the tip-top and it rolled down the line and the coils lying at my feet pulled up through the guides and out into the air. The line reached its curling finger out and out and out until the line end disappeared up the guides and out the tip-top. "Awesome," I whispered.

"Having fun, mate?" Peter the guide said. "Let's be after those trout, then." He had shouldered his rucksack and stood waiting to be off on the trail that led along a tumbling freestoner up the distant valley into a New Zealand alpine wilderness.

Despite the urge to be off and after the trout of dreams, I made one or two more casts. I wanted to feel the magic, to play the music that lies within a fine rod.

How often have I heard the guides' wailing wall complaint: "If only they could cast; what fishing they could have." Good casting is to fly fishing what the swing is to golfing: There can be no success without it. It had taken me twenty years of mistakes to learn the lessons of strength, timing, and mental control in casting. I had tried strength first, convinced that power made distance casting what it is—the delivery of energy to the line through the rod. It slowly dawned on me, after I reached the first magic distance of sixty feet, that something was wrong with my entire approach to good casting. It would take the instruction of Mel Krieger and Lefty Kreh to undo my mistakes. I had to swallow pride and begin from scratch, forget casting shibboleths and reprogram my muscle memories from wrong to right.

It took about two years to learn the basics properly. Then I discovered another fundamental lesson—practice. For some unfathomable reason fly fishers will not practice the most fundamental aspect of their sport—casting. I discovered, through my associations with the greatest casters of our day—including Steve Rajeff, Jerry Siem, Joan and Lee Wulff, and others—that they practice, practice, and practice. Like professional golfers, they work at their skills. I began to practice.

I set out measured distances for myself on my back lawn—a peg at thirty feet, the next at sixty, and then a third at ninety feet, near the end of the lawn. I began by casting for tight loops. I controlled myself: I would cast no greater distance until the loop in the backcast and the forward cast was tight. I began at thirty feet, then moved quickly to forty, then fifty, then sixty and seventy. It was coming. I could see how important a stiff wrist was in loop control. Then I learned to keep the rod in plane in both the backcast and forward cast. Jerry Siem told me it had taken him *a decade* to perfect simply his *backcast,* with practice sessions every day, and following his advice, I learned the patience of the professional athlete.

I began to catch more fish. It slowly dawned on me that the Golden Door of fly fishing is casting, accurate casting. It also became obvious to me that good distance casting, with heavy lines, is different from short, accurate tip casting. South Florida guides sling line the way Lefty Kreh slings line—long and fast and accurately. I watched Lefty sling heavy lines all day without the slightest fatigue. Using a tight overhand stroke, I could not cast all day without extreme fatigue and, finally, tennis elbow. I altered my stroke, took an off-shoulder stab to the rear, and learned the short, fast haul that produces the classic Kreh sling. Then I read about the same technique recommended forty years ago by Ellis Newman and Al McClane.

The magic came to me. I felt it in my arms and shoulders. I discovered the inherent character that lies deep within the great rods. I discovered how to bring that character out and test it in the backyard and on the stream. I learned to approach each rod on its own terms, to listen to what it has to say. I discovered slowly that the great rod makers have brought grapite, epoxy, scrim, and tapers together to create rods that speak purposefully to the great casters the way great violins speak to great violinists. Expert casters know how to make great rods speak and perform eloquently. And the communication between great rods and great casters is a delight to witness. To experience this delight is to enter one room of the fly fisher's Tenth Level mansion.

I learned that casting is also a state of mind, one that can reach Zen-like importance to the fly fisher. We enter this state when we are alone, casting in sync with the universe on a quiet stream at dusk, and there is such sensual delight that we abandon ourselves to our casting and almost hope that the fish will ignore our fly. This is the Tenth Level, where sport is defined by the physical and emotional poetry of perfection.

We headed upriver at a fast pace set by Peter. He had first earned his living as a professional helicopter deer shooter, but the business had died and now for three hundred dollars a day he hunted big trout for wealthy Americans. Peter had one good eye and beside it a perfect glass match. But the glass eye did not move, so the composite effect was a little weird. You never knew which eye to look at when talking to him. You'd start out comfortably and looking at his left eye, but then you'd get an uneasy feeling that the eye wasn't really looking back at you and you'd have to shift over to the right eye and work that one for a while, ultimately a little skeptical about whether it was the control eye or not. It made you damned edgy. You worried about talking to Peter, but you wanted to talk to him because he was so nice, a real Kiwi. And he knew so much about trout.

When Peter stepped off up that river trail the bottom line of our predicament became clear. He didn't walk the trail; he ate it the way a greyhound devours a racetrack. And he expected Jack and me to keep up. Jack gave me one of those quick looks that says *Oh shit!* I returned it and jumped into high gear.

"Hold up a minute," Jack wheezed after I'd halted a mile up the trail, breathing hard, not seeing Peter anywhere ahead and waiting for Jack to catch up.

"Just give me a minute to rest here. What's the hurry, anyway?"

Jack was a successful salesman from Milwaukee. His traveling companion had whispered to me, "Jack's no fly fisherman really. Can't cast for shit. You'll like him, though. And he'll probably give you most of the shots at the fish."

"Come on, Jack," I said. "If we don't keep up with this guy there won't be any fishing. He knows where the fish are. Listen, let's agree that you take the first fish, and me the second, and so on. That's fair, isn't it?"

"Yeah, no problem. Let's go."

By the time we reached the great stand of beeches, he was sweating and huffing and insisted on halting again. Peter waited up the trail among the beeches, intently watching the river. We stood panting in the cool hush of the gray columnar beeches that ran in elegant hallways from the gothic cliffs and alpine pastures down to the river.

The guide motioned urgently. We were still panting when we reached his side.

"Down!" Peter ordered with an urgent hand signal.

We dropped to all fours then knelt behind him like two obedient, panting setters.

"See them there, mates? See the one there just above the willow? He'd be about five pound. The second one up's about three and his nibs there at the head'll go close to ten. Right then, mates? Let's take a blow. Get our thoughts together and then have a go."

"God, look at those fish, Jack!" I said. "If you take the down-stream one by the willow first and don't spook the others, I can catch the next and then you the third! We can clean house!"

"What's the best thing to do here?" Jack said. "I'm not exactly sure I can reach that fish."

"Hell, it's only forty feet, Jack! It's a setup."

I was beginning to wish I'd kept the first fish for myself. If he blew the fish, he might spook them all, a wipeout.

"Have you done much fly fishing then, Jack?" Peter inquired, his left eye unblinkingly scrutinizing Jack's equipment.

"Well, I've done my share, but that cast looks tricky. How close can we get to the fish?"

"Listen, mate. I can get you in close from below the trout. I want you to stay low in a crouch. We'll ease up along the bank. See how they're feeding there? They feel good about things. We just want to keep them that way, okay? I'd tie on a Royal Wulff, Jack, about a 16 with good wire if you've got one. If you hook that fish he's gonna bust right for that willow. You've got to turn him downstream or he's a goner. And if he gets upstream, he'll spook those other two fish for sure."

The rocks clattered as the two fishermen picked their way down the little talus slope to the stream. Peter tiptoed with Jack imitating his moves through the purple-topped thistles.

The guide crouched and sneaked to the waterside just below the willow. Jack held back, kneeling and nervously checking his fly, line, and reel. He whispered something that was lost in the sound of the stream. Peter looked back and motioned to come up. The trout fed happily, moving sideways in the currents to take the drifting nymphs. Watching from the hill, I thought, *So this is it, man against big trout, in a small, clear stream. Let the game begin!*

Peter whispered something over his shoulder and Jack lifted his rod and the line into a short false cast. The fly caught in a thistletop behind him and I heard a low curse. He crawled back to the thistle and retrieved the fly. I heard Peter whisper something. Jack lifted the rod again and glanced over his shoulder to watch the backcast. It sailed into the thistle. He retrieved it. Peter whispered, this time for about a minute, and his arm came up and back in a casting motion.

The fish fed on above the willow, but they were ranging less. It was as if they had sensed something different, but were not quite sure what. Perhaps they thought that sheep had come down to the stream to drink—something that would make familiar ground vibrations but not threaten them. I thought, *Who knows what goes on in a trout's little brain? They're feeding machines, really.*

Peter whispered something again and Jack lifted his rod and the line came up and back above the thistles and then forward and crashed to the surface on the trout's head. The fish bolted upstream, careening wildly through the other two. They dashed for the brush. The stream was empty.

Peter glanced at Jack, then turned and stalked up the bank. Jack said something to him, then shrugged and followed him through the thistles and up to where I stood examining the knots in my leader.

"What could I have done?" he said. "I couldn't cast from where he put me. Those fish are too spooky, anyway, don'tcha think? God, didja see how they lit out of there?"

Peter's right eye was blinking and twitching as he turned and stalked off upriver. I decided it was in fact his real eye. I vowed I would address it exclusively, and respectfully, when speaking to him.

I worried about facing the next fish, and I thought for a long time about the guides' lament—"if only they could cast."

Chapter Four

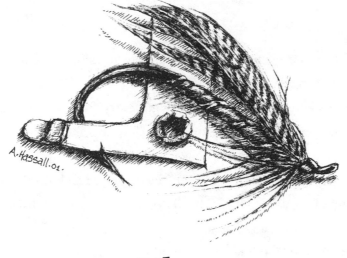

A. Hassall. 01.

Flies

There is an Old World resort on Little Averill Lake in northern Vermont where the cottages are named for the grand flies of fly fishing's gilded age. As you walk by them on a stroll to the main pine-paneled dining room, the cottage names are a memory lane roll call to a fly fisher: Silver Doctor, Parmachene Belle, Warden's Worry, Royal Wulff, Rusty Rat, Mickey Finn, Nine Three, Montreal. Most are named for the multicolored streamers of the lake's glory days, when time hung suspended like a glistening drop of dew on a spiderweb and deep-bellied brookies and lake trout lay waiting for the fishermen in the clean, blue-gray waters of the Averills.

The sports who brought their families to this place were city professionals for whom leisure time was an inherited right of class. The clean, fine-grain black-and-white prints of their family in the album here tell the story. How relaxed and together the families look despite their stiff Victorian collars, their full-length dresses, and that air of immaculate period whiteness.

The father, standing prim and tall beside a grand LaSalle touring car, *was* father, the core of the "family unit." Strange. Now that the family is disappearing, we invent a term to describe its lost glory. In these photos it is visible. A young girl in a sailor's-uniform dress stands proudly by her pony—mornings were spent on horseback. Mother holds a croquet mallet. A checked picnic tablecloth lies on the ground and children, aunts, and uncles recline in a self-conscious, relaxed, and stylized—patrician—pose. The fathers in these photos tied and fished the grand flies for which the cottages have been named.

Time at this resort hangs suspended like a bee buzzing in a drowsy autumn garden. There are croquet wickets on the lodge's well-kept lawn, and in the Victorian gardens fieldstone walks meander to nowhere, and beckon. It is a place to dawdle, to stop and smell and listen, to wile away the hours "in sweet dalliance," a phrase, and an idea, lost in time.

Suspended beside the path in a shaft of liquid sunlight is a glowing amber blown-glass vial. From its tiny delicate spout a shining drop of clear fluid hangs enticingly, as though ripe and ready to fall. The air whirs gently and a small, precise, airborne figure darts to the vial and halts in a neat midair pirouette. Its wings move so rapidly that they are invisible. It is a ruby-throated hummingbird, come from the surrounding woods to drink.

Others join it in the air. They are proud birds: polite, elegant, aloof, perhaps even cultured. They hold, patiently waiting their turns at the droplet feeder. Holding, holding, a bird rotates slightly left, then right, exercising a very precise, and neat, control of itself and the air while, slightly impatient, queuing up for the honeyed droplet.

When its turn has come, the bird approaches the bead of liquid, halts, flits backward, suspended, forward, backward, forward. Its long curved beak seems to touch, but not touch, the droplet. A high-speed photo would show its astoundingly long, thin tongue snaking out to touch the globule of sweetened water as it gently, cleanly, and gracefully siphons the liquid into its body. I imagine Audrey Hepburn sipping an aperitif at the Plaza.

The hummingbirds are part of the garden. They belong there in the druidic drone of the bee wings and the sweet-smelling blossoms, the lawns that smell of freshly mown grass, and the cottages named for legendary fishing flies.

Everything about this place is suspended in time—the way it was. The way life should be. When I am here, I wish to be a Victorian country man, a fly tier and fly fisher, what Steve Bodio has called "a member of a semi-esoteric, exclusive brotherhood linked by shared passions and arcane knowledge" . . . and wealth. All this garden requires is a kindly garden-tending grandmother to make it perfect. *But*, I wonder uneasily, *where has my grandfather's world gone—have we traded it for a market-based consumer economy?*

The flies, so elegant, their names so evocative of fishing history and lore, are the angling dressage of this resort. They, too, are of another, quiet and elegant era when a fly fisher had time to sit at the tying vise and reflect, to create with exotic feathers the opulent, rococo offerings of yesteryear, what Lee Wulff described as "the fly fisher's gift to the fish."

Junglecock, African bustard, polar bear hair. How absolutely rare, innocent, self-indulgent, and, well, wasteful, they seem today. In the faces of these Victorian photos I see no suspicion that it will end—this world of exotic feathers and fur—that it can quite literally be used up. They are unaware that the exquisite self-indulgent certainty of their lives, so serene in their expressions, will disappear.

When I hold one of these wonderful flies in my hand, I am transported back into the fly tier's world. It is a Victorian place, like the garden, where flies are elegantly dressed and laid gently in highly polished leather wallets lined with lambskin. Fly lines are silken and must be dressed and cared for before and after fishing. Leaders are of silkworm gut, drawn straight between the teeth of Spanish women sitting in sweatshops. They must be retained in dampened packets of felt to keep them soft for fishing. These ceremonials were important to fly fishers.

The flies are overly dressed, for, as the commercial tier of the day understood, *sparsely tied flies catch fish; heavily dressed flies hook fishermen in the wallet.*

The flies of the rich are richly dressed with the exotic materials from all corners of the British Empire. The salmon flies of Victorian England are the high gothic creations of fly tying. Extraordinarily ornate, graceful, and overly elegant, they reek of upper-class elegance. Kelson is the high priest of this wonderful salmon-fly culture. His book, *The Salmon Fly,* lovingly hand-illustrated, is the cult bible.

And so it goes, descending culturally into the plebeian flies of the world. Less elegant and presumptuous, but no less effective, these flies reflect their backgrounds of place, time, function, and social suspension.

The flies of the North American backwoods are often made of abundant animal hair—deer, elk, moose—and feathers. The winter hairs of these animals are hollow; thus they provide exceptional flotation, a requirement of effective dry flies. The flies (both wet and dry) were also inexpensive to create: The animals and birds from which they came populated the unexploited American Eden from Maine to the Upper Peninsula of Michigan and across Canada to the Rockies and the Cascades. Little wonder, then, that the practical artifice of the wet fly was born where the fish are, in the remote woods, lakes, and streams of the country. Their elegant city cousins were ornate, egocentric offerings. And, as with writing and the visual arts, the flies were always the crafty expression of the tier's hopes, his desires, and, ultimately, his attempt to imitate nature, clutch fate, and capture immortality. They were also, as Tom McGuane has noted, ". . . the product of avid reflection as to what a predator ought to do with his prey in a manner complimentary to the destiny of each." A trout or salmon might shrink from that notion, for as Paul Schullery has cautioned us: "Would we fish if a trout could shriek in ter-ror?" Modern anthropomorphism has crept into our conscious-ness, so much so that hookless flies have become the obsession of at least one well-known fly tier. His fulfillment attends the rise to his imitation and a momentary tug on the line. His ethics will allow him no more.

The early American wet flies were for trolling, designed to be pulled through water and to look like swimming baitfish. They also worked well in the moving waters of streams, where the pull of the water moved the fly and gave it life. The form of the flies was thus determined by their function. But though the country fisherman cared little for elegance, and could seldom afford ex-otic materials, his flies were creations of great beauty, sometimes rising to the level of near-art, though few tiers considered art as an end in their tying.

Dry flies came later in their development in North America. And the dry-fly-tying craft flowered slowly in the North Woods, where hatches were, and are, sparse and episodic, lasting reliably only from late April to mid-June. Farther south, in the Catskills and the Pennsylvania limestone country, where the mayfly biota is more vibrant and its hatches last throughout the summer and into fall, the American craft of the dry fly and its fishing had its birth and its epitome. The inspiration came from England and flowered slowly in the East, sending its seeds westward to the upper Midwest, the Rockies, and the West Coast.

Nothing is more elegant in creation than a dry fly and the insect that it imitates. Its form follows its function: to float and look like a water-born insect and to catch the trout that will rise to eat it. The fly tiers of the Catskills discovered that a sparsely dressed, heavily hackled fly floated well and caught trout on the riffles and glides of their streams. The "Catskill tie" became a classic of the American tying streamcraft, a functional creation designed by experienced fly fishers to catch wild trout in the Catskill streams.

Pennsylvania fly fishers who fished the Pocono Mountains for trout created similar flies, as did the fly fishers of the Cumberland Valley streams of Pennsylvania. But it soon became clear to a few Cumberland Valley limestone spring-creek fishers that their prolonged summer hatches consisted of smaller mayflies: to match them would require sparsely tied, tiny flies that floated low in the surface film. Gradually the modern dry-fly era was born and its innovators—Gordon,

Flies

Christian, Steenrod, Jennings, Hewitt, Bergman, the Dettes, the Darbees, Schwiebert, Flick, Harvey, Marinaro, Fox, and Caucci and Nastasi; and, in the upper Midwest, Blades, Swisher and Richards, and Borger—developed fly-tying techniques to create more killing drys for their waters. Though they worked apart, these legends of American fly fishing worked together to create more effective flies. The dry-fly tiers were aided in the 1950s by Harry Darbee's backyard hit-or-miss development of genetic hackle, which finally, with the opening of a commercial "hackle farm" by Bucky Metz in Pennsylvania, provided dry-fly tiers with the stiff hackle that gave us the high-floating modern dry fly.

As American fly fishers moved westward, they took their dressings with them—and changed them to meet new stream and lake conditions. The Eastern dressings worked well on trout (and later steelhead and salmon) in Michigan and Minnesota because the rivers had flows similar to the valley streams of the East and similar hatches. But fly fishers in the Rockies soon discovered that their turbulent runoff flows required more fly flotation and thus heavier dressings. Their gentle valley spring-creek flows demanded other fly forms, similar to the small-fly dressings suited to the slow-moving limestone streams of Pennsylvania, where trout sip leisurely and inspect their food before taking. The fly forms changed to meet the conditions and the no-hackles, which Swisher and Richards had introduced in Michigan, had a new birth on the spring creeks of western Montana and Idaho. Rene Harrop, inspired by Swisher and Richards, created spring-creek emerger imitations; Gary LaFontaine and Al Troth hatched caddis imitations; and George Grant haunted the Big Hole River with his woven flies.

The Northwest steelheaders heard a different drummer. Jim Pray, Tommy Brayshaw, Syd Glasso, Harry Lemire, Enos Bradner, Walt Johnson, and others began their fishing with traditional Atlantic salmon flies, then blazed their own paths to create innovative streamers and drys for both winter and summer steelhead.

From the era of Walton and Cotton to this day one value has remained contemporary: In the fly is the fly fisher. When I view the flies of Marinaro, I see the fishing values and ambitions of the man who tied them. In the Kelson, Blades, Pray, Flick, Harvey, or Schwiebert flies lie the values, hopes, skills, and experiences of the men who worked alone—yet together—at their vises, borrowing a technique or a material here, inventing something there, and each jealously protecting his turf. In his own private way the fly tier is immortal: In his creations his values outlive him. He takes me by the hand to fish his fish on his stream, to live his dreams. His flies, as McGuane has observed, "reveal a poetic intuition for breaking down the watery walls" that lie between us and the fish. He is the hunter who will bring his dream to the surface, where it will be enticed to take, and caught, and held . . . and released.

Wulff worked wonders with animal hair, and his flies will endure because they will always catch fish on the salmon streams and trout rivers of the world. Lefty's Deceivers, shaped from long brilliantly colored saddle hackles, will survive him, for they match the baitfish of the world. Troth's Elk Hair Caddis will occupy every fly box because it imitates the ubiquitous caddis in black, green, and tan and because it casts without helicoptering and floats like a cork.

Sit still for a while on a quiet Labrador lake and watch the *Isonychia* nymphs wiggle their way to the surface and you will appreciate the creations of Fred Arbona, Ken Iwamasa, and others. Fish the night for large trout and you will soon discover the large winged streamers created by George Harvey and Joe Humphreys. Fish for bass and Dave Whitlock's hair creations will help you understand why large lunches catch big fish—because his flies have large profiles, move water, have colors that trigger fish to attack, and look like food that bass eat.

The invention of long nylon hairlike filaments allowed Bob Popovics, working with epoxy to bind the material, to create large baitfish imitations that are relatively easy to cast in the wind. These flies have revolutionized saltwater fly tying and fishing. And the techniques used to tie them are invading the world of freshwater fishing thanks to tiers such as Scott Sanchez, D. L. Goddard, and others.

Many of the exotic materials that created the flamboyantly colored Atlantic salmon streamers of Victorian times are now banned from importation, but tying the flies with new acceptable materials has become a passion for tiers worldwide. In fact, Paul Schmookler—author (and publisher) with Ingrid Sils of *Rare and Unusual Fly Tying Materials, Volumes I and II*—estimates that fifty thousand people tie them but do not fish. (The flies are tied primarily for display.) The salmon-fly-tying passion has been nurtured by Schmookler and Sills, Bill Hunter, Wayne Luallen, John Van Der Hoof, Dave McNeese, Mike Martinek Jr., Mark Waslik, and others, bringing new life to the original creations of George M. Kelson, Francis Francis, and, later, Charles

Defeo and Michel Rogan. Michael Frodin's *Classic Salmon Flies, History and Patterns* (1991) tells the story.

The creation of North America's first homegrown two-handed rods by the Sage Rod Company using a Jimmy Green design in the 1980s introduced European salmon-fishing techniques to North America, and steelhead fishermen were the first to adapt them to the rivers of the Northwest. They allowed anglers to swim and skitter flies more effectively than they had ever been fished before. During the same period rapidly improving hook-manufacturing processes provided fly tiers with chemically sharpened hooks and designs that made tying easier and flies more functional. Since then egg imitations have been added to the steelheader's traditional streamers, and heavily hackled waking flies have become increasingly popular for fishing summer steelhead thanks to the influence of Lani Waller and Bill McMillan. And the traditional steelhead wets have grown in popularity thanks to innovative marabou and rabbit-strip patterns created by Northwest steelheaders.

Bob Clouser took a simple hook, turned it upside down, tied in dumbbell eyes to make it ride hook-up, added deer hair, and called it a Deep Minnow. It became one of the world's most popular flies because big fish feed near the bottom and they feed on baitfish, which the Deep Minnow imitates. But fly tiers refuse to rest on their successes. Innovations to the Clouser continue to emerge, with flash added and eyes moved forward and backward along the hook shank to create more wounded baitfish motions, and imitations are now tied in every shade and color. Inevitably, legs will change the "original" Clouser again.

Rubber legs are just the latest wrinkle in flies. They have been around since long before the Girdle Bug came off the vise, but they have now changed even the lowly ant. Fly tiers laughed when the first foam Chernobyl Ant appeared. They stopped when the "fly" took trout faster than any terrestrial imitation of modern times. Since then foam has become the body material of preference for tying ants and beetles, and the material has also invaded the mayfly imitation world. If you are a purist you may choke a little, but you cannot stop these invasions.

Who would have predicted the arrival of flies tied with gold or silver metal, and later plastic, beads on their heads? They emigrated from Europe, where they were designed by Roman Moser. In the 1980s they were reported to American tiers by Tom Rosenbauer, and in the two years following their introduction, the bead-head nymph display cases overran American fly shops. Nymphing has never been the same, and fly rods have paid the price, with tip-tops pitted from the impacts of weighted flies. Unlimited rod warranties were introduced as an answer to increasing rod breakage. Conehead flies? Who would have thunk it?

Could Bergman foresee the ass of the duck as a source of more effective tying feathers? Cul de canard feathers, when applied to a hook, create cunning impressions of mayfly and midge emergers that trout find irresistible, and the flies seem to float forever without flotant.

I belong now to the honorable order of terminally hooked fly-tying junkies. I avoid certain fly shops because I cannot refrain from buying *any* new material. Each winter I attend Bob Clouser's fly-tying classes once a week. It's so good to be there, listening to stories, learning and sharing new techniques, and discovering new materials, that I am frustrated when I must skip a gathering: Perhaps I will *miss* something. Now my house is filled with flies and materials threaten to overrun my den and my wife grumbles and mumbles about wafting feather fuzz and hooks in the carpeting. My Feng Shui is crumbling under this mass of stuff; I must get organized!

Becoming a Fly Fisher

—

68

Back in the 1950s I suspected that Jim Deren's Angler's Roost in New York City had to be the roost of the truly demented. Now I know that it was the place where a fly tier could find wondrous materials that he could lash to hooks to create the lifelike objects of his devotion, his gifts to the fish. I've just heard about a newly created dyed squirrel fur from Wapsi that reflects a blue sheen that makes rainbows commit suicide. I've heard that John Betts and John Barr are working on deadly new flies. I think I will call to pick their brains. Otherwise I might miss something.

Chapter Five

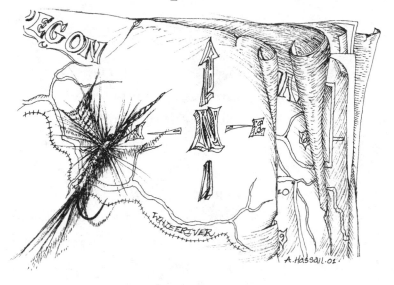

Places

I shall be telling this with a sigh

Somewhere ages and ages hence;

Two roads diverged in a yellow wood and I—

I took the one less traveled by,

And that has made all the difference.

Robert Frost

"The Road Not Taken"

Frost Poems

The places that we fly fish provide us with mystical connections. They are natural paradigms of life's need for form and meaning. They make us question: Is our identity a dream—are we process or reality? Are we, like ephemera, like the nymph, just an instar? Are forms an illusion of the time dimension, each individually clinging to its present nature? Is the mayfly a transcendant lesson? I recall that while I hunt for North Carolina redfish sun devils loom on spartina grass flats. They are evanescent visitations of light appearing like hope a long way off at the meeting of sky and earth.

I also have discovered on certain streams, when the atmospherics conspire, that a slight elevation in the humidity hovering above the water's surface mysteriously calls the green drake. We think that the rainbow, unsuccessfully, attempts to attach itself to the earth; where the green drake hatch emerges around me it succeeds. Perhaps these are just brief almanacs of Nature's hidden intent. But to me these happenings, appearing on homeless frontiers, illumine the precipitous edges where things become. My experiences are important and personal, but they are also joyous communions shared by all fly fishers. They inspire our happiness.

THE BIG HOLE

You can sit on the deck at the lodge and look a long way up the Big Hole River. About a mile upstream you can see a fisherman exploring things for himself. Beyond him the river rounds a bend and disappears below a column of red sandstone, afire in the evening glow.

Below the deck a short cast away trout dimple where a spring creek enters the murmuring river. Martins knife above the water like hungry spirits. The whole place has an enchanting feel about it, as though a rift has opened in the mountains to reveal a secret Shangri-la.

Do such places truly exist? This one certainly does, and as fly tier George Grant discovered decades ago, to view such a stream is to be forever possessed by it. Perhaps it is the deep slot that leads into the Big Hole valley that creates the feeling of a special hidy place. Suddenly you emerge from the canyon and the valley bursts upon you before your senses have time to adjust to vaulting peaks and soaring spires with a river running through it. No matter how many times you see it, you swear that it is yours alone, that you are the first one to see the secret place. It must be yours, you tell yourself, for no one else could possibly see it exactly as you do.

Nonsense, perhaps. But one cannot change human nature, and the Big Hole, like other great rivers, is possessive. High on its little tributary, the Wise River, the early-morning air is so cold you can swallow it like springwater, so fresh it tastes clean like new wine. A spire of rock plunges a thousand feet to the sparkling little stream. A little rainbow smacks your first cast and you are off. Nothing much seems important after that except trout, water, and sunlight that fills the world.

The Big Hole River itself is a fine place, full of brookies, rainbows, browns, cutthroats, and grayling high up in the sweet-grass meadows. The wading is treacherous, though, and I have floated my hat below the Wise River Club. I have staggered dripping from the river and sat to dry in the warm August sun while watching rising trout, after a while slipping back into the flow to have at them again. Nothing ever seemed quite so good as being there, alone.

Downstream the river dives left before tumbling into the canyon where the big trout live. Just before dark a fine caddis hatch brings them up to feed, dimpling here and there between the walls of rock. A big trout bulges the water and gentle rings radiate out toward the canyon walls. A tiddler launches itself at a caddis; a bank feeder nudges his nose into the surface film and wallows gently with his head working in deliberate gluttony.

Finally, when we float, the chilly dusk in the canyon clutches us and we must shoulder our sweaters. The cold seeps in along our necks as the rower dodges the dory down through the rocks and chutes to the pullout below the washed-out stone power-house. The night air has turned chillier than I can ever remember, and as we haul out my back and arm muscles ache from the fishing and wading. Ahead the lights of the lodge appear against the inky black of the river behind it. Inside are white table-cloths, shiny long-stemmed glasses, and a rack of lamb served with a green salad and the river murmuring beyond the deck. A glimpse of the lone figure wading upriver I know I shall recall twenty years hence, a Big Hole riverman . . . fishing.

LETORT SPRING RUN

It was dusk by the time we reached the bridge above the quarry. Ground fog settled into the little Letort Spring Run valley as we walked downstream to the footbridge and halted to search the water. Nervous water in the quiet bridge pool betrayed a trout restlessly in search of food. His dorsal appeared for a second and then disappeared. Downstream another trout patrolled the tailwater of the next pool, and so it went in the little limestone spring creek: The trout, feeling safe in the darkness, were going on the fin.

In my excitement to thread the line and leader up the rod guides I missed the sixth guide. The turle knot would not tie in the darkness, and I settled for an improved clinch. As I stepped onto the spongy quaking ground at streamside and crouched to sneak close for a cast to the cruising trout below the bridge, a knifing bow wave shot from the shallow gravel tailwater and ran upstream to the dark and sheltered nooks and crannies of the bridge. *Tout finis.*

I tried the next downstream fish—*adios!* I schlepped in among the high weeds for a shot at the third. I knee-walked to casting distance and backcast high and caught goldenrod. I ripped the fly free and lifted the tippet to the wan sky to check it—gone. I thought of Nick Lyons. I fumbled in my pockets for the right fly box and after four pockets recalled that it was in the duffel at home, still resting from the Montana trip. I settled for a ratty fly-patch Muddler and fumbled in the darkness with flip-focals and tippets and a hook eye that had obviously closed since the fly's last use. Trout wakes slanted here and there in the spring run while I fumbled in the weeds and watched.

There! The tippet finally poked through the hook eye and the Muddler snugged down and held firmly when I pulled on it. I knee-walked closer to the run. Just enough light left to spot the outline of a cress bed. I cast the fly beside it and let the pattern sink and sweep downcurrent. It stopped and I lifted the rod tip gently. Live weight wriggled down the line. The trout, a big one, thrashed and rolled a rod length away. I led the fish into a bed of cress at my knees and lifted gently and rolled it on its side.

The brilliant pink stripe along the brown's flanks glowed in the falling light. It occurred to me that it was the most brilliantly colored wild brown I had ever seen. Its head was large for a twenty-inch fish, but its stomach was full and deep. It might go three pounds, I thought, as I turned the trout and examined it. A diet of spring-creek scuds and cress bugs had colored the fish with vivid stripes, which extended along its gill covers and down its flanks to just above its ventral fins.

The brown's markings were distinctly different from the butter-yellow, halo-spotted fish I had taken previously on the Letort. As I examined it, I considered the brilliance of trout colors in cold, clean scud-filled spring creeks. I recalled radiantly colored fish taken on such streams as Darlington Ditch, Thompson's, Nelson's, and Armstrong's. They are fragile streams that cannot endure much pounding by fishermen. They are often privately held, and the landowner's affection for trout and fly fishing leads him to be protectively paranoid about his water and its fish.

Spring creeks are the crown jewels of the North American trout streams. Their welfare requires special handling, with limited and controlled access by fishermen and regulations that call for sport fishing only. They are best protected by single owners who allow a limited number of fishermen on their beats, and then only under tight prescriptions of sporting conduct. Others survive under careful fishing-regulation management by the state, but their futures are always subject to destruction by land-use changes in their watersheds.

That evening, after I released the trout and returned home, my local newspaper reported heartening news. The Letort Spring Run—where Marinaro and Charlie Fox pursued their personal muses—would be considered for designation as a Pennsylvania Scenic River. Now included in the program, the little spring creek, which is surrounded by increasing development, may survive as a premier trout stream into the twenty-first century, although under continued assault by developers.

It occurred to me then that I had taken and released the brown almost on the spot where Vince Marinaro had kept his fishing tent, at the spot where the Interstate 81 bridge now crosses the Letort. I recalled his discussions of that place in his *Modern Dry Fly Code* and his long fight to preserve the limestoner.

DEVIL'S GAP

The Devil's Gap is a mile-long salmon pool on the Eagle River in Labrador. Like many of the great Atlantic salmon pools in the world, it has a special capacity for holding fish. At the head of the pool, where the tea-colored water creates foam lines along a smooth gneiss ledge, you can sit and watch the salmon nose into the currents. They plane up as if to sniff the water's surface, then disappear into its depths. It is pleasing to see them there, and if one stays long and watches closely, he can educate himself in the ways that salmon frolic.

Salmon seem to be at play when they hold so closely packed together in the oxygen-rich foam. They poke their noses up against the underwater rock over which the main flow sluices and hold there in clean, nearly symmetrical ranks. Their backs are blue-black blending down to silver sides, then into snow-white bellies. Their noses are pointed, and when they tip up into the foam line, they frisk as though riding a water slide. A salmon in the ranks suddenly shoots forward and up and breaks the surface, sometimes leaping high or just skimming and flashing on its side. The rest hold their places during the performance, like a patient audience, each member waiting its turn on stage.

These fish can be caught. The fishermen dap their flies to skitter them across the surface over the salmon. Occasionally a fish moves slightly when the fly crosses his viewing window. He's interested. Sometimes a salmon rises to intercept the fly but just kisses it before returning to his place in the fish echelon. And then a fish rises sharply and takes, and the angler lifts from high on the rocks above, and the fight is on. The fish makes a shiny splinter in the sun, then a great echoing splash into the amber water.

Men are mesmerized by this watching and dapping and hooking of salmon. They stand for hours without moving, their eyes fixed on the fish and the fly. I am transfixed, too, but I need wading and casting and stepping at the pool's tailout to feel that I am actually salmon fishing. Yet I am drawn back again and again to watch the fish. I have seldom had such an opportunity to observe unusual, intimate salmon behavior.

In the evening I slip down to the tail of the mile-long pool for a flick of the fly. Far upriver I can see the dappers. One rod bends deeply; the fisherman holds his arms high and a glint of silver appears in the dark air above the pool. I cast Tom Humphrey's

Eagle's Nest fly alongside a ledge at the tailout, not six feet from my rod tip. The fly swings in tight to the ledge and stops against something hard.

I have no time to set the hook. In a determined take the fish turns and runs downstream toward the Class IV rapids. It leaps once, then again, and again. It takes seventy yards of backing before nearing the throat of the rapids, but before it can dash into whitewater, I drop the rod tip and strip line. The salmon pauses as though pondering whether to plunge downriver. I reel in line until it goes taut. Then I reel in, slowly, tightening, and put the rod over my shoulder and walk the fish upriver until I lead it safely into calmer water.

Minutes later I have a twelve-pound hen in my hands.

ON THE FLATS

It is a windless, flat-calm morning. To the northwest thunderheads have begun to build beyond Florida Bay, perhaps in the Glades behind Flamingo, where as a boy I first saw a redfish and a tarpon and my father floated, and lost, his bait box.

The sky here is mirrored on the water's glassy surface and the image is so perfect that sky and horizon meld into one. It is a pensile atmospheric zone for the bonefish hunter, who feels physically suspended, cut from his moorings as though imagination and reality have fused. The guide poles while your eyes search for something, a line tracing the silklike surface, a tail or a dorsal. You listen for a distant splash. A leopard ray, frightened by the boat, slices away, its belly flashing white. The air hangs hot and limpid and bonefish fantasies overtake you as you strain to see through the surface glare with amber-lensed polaroids. The birds—pelicans, egrets, and herons—have taken to the mangrove islands, where they squabble and annoy each other. The cormorants sit on mile markers, patiently awaiting a tide change and nervously fidgeting when the boat passes. On the flats of the world at dead low tide the creatures wait for the onset of the young flood. And you wait, too, caught in a limbo of intense glare, stillness, and the uneasy apprehension that all life has been suspended, and your hopes for an encounter have vanished. By noon your head aches and your knees burn and your back throbs from catlike hunching, intense searching, and unfulfilled anticipation.

A bonefish at first glimpse gets little respect from a trout fisherman, for its shape is shockingly suckerlike and vulpine. From its head peer absurdly large, mirrorlike eyes that seem perpetually surprised and innocent. Surrounding its small mouth are tough, chubby, circular lips that conceal strong bonelike crushers within its throat for pulverizing the snails, crabs, and other small shell-fish that it sucks from the flats bottom and mangrove roots.

A healthy bonefish of thirty inches carries the belly of a fat man; it will overflow your fingers when you grasp it. Thirty-inch-plus bones are trophies; thirty-three-inch-plus fish raise pulses; thirty-five-inch-plus Biscayne Bay Specials win world records.

After the trout fisherman recovers from his first encounter with a bonefish, after he hooks up, he is changed by three things: how fast and how long the fish can run (it may be the first time this fisherman has seen his backing), and how perfectly designed it is for syphoning the flats bottom. If he learns to love bonefish, he may haunt those places where they feed and he may, gradu-ally, discover the intricate solunar web of life on the tidal flats, where the oceans gently touch the land.

He will need a guide for his explorations, for this ebb-and-flow world, the interface between the sea and the land, is tempermen-tal. One tide enters here and another remains dead low a mile away; bones contour one flat at six inches of flood and on another at three. He will learn that timing the tides to meet the fish on each flat requires the guide's sixth sense, an intuition for which he is paid well.

Without an experienced guide all is hit or miss—luck. And with him, behind and on the poling platform, the trout fisherman for the first time becomes a lowly team player. He must quickly forge a relationship with the man who controls the boat and who is the captain of all he surveys—Ahab and quarterback all in one.

Some Florida Keys bonefish guides have in previous careers been Marine drill instructors. Others *think* they have. All expect fast performance. None tolerates poor casting. Few condone tardiness or a reluctance to take sudden and sharp commands.

"Let's go. I know a flat that gets an early young incoming," Bob says. The Yamaha kicks us up on step and we race over a close bottom spread like a multicolored onrushing carpet of turtle grass, sea fans, starfish, and propeller scars. Surprised rays dash to the left and right. We cross channels, skim alongside mangrove islands, and enter mysterious basins, and then stop suddenly to stand silently and eyeball their intimate shallows for moving shapes, dorsals or tails.

"They're here," Bob whispers. Small round holes dot the flats bottom, and there is a milky cast to the clear water drifting toward the mangrove shallows.

Places

—

"You can wade this flat. If I pole in along that point you can fish downlight. They'll be feeding into the incoming toward you. I usually find big fish on this flat. Try that Size 4 weedless Merkin I gave you. Wade slowly; they'll spook in this skinny water."

Bob poles along the point and stops to let me slide into five inches of clear, tepid water. He stands on the poling tower, peering down the flat. I tie on the Merkin and check the knot and strip line. I hold the hook bend between my thumb and forefinger and trail the line behind me as I wade across coral sand at the edge of the marl bottom.

"Look up near the mangroves. There's something moving there; it might be a tailer," Bob yells. I move forward, tense now with the anticipation of an encounter and the fear of blowing a shot at a large bonefish.

"See him, now?" Bob asks.

"Yes, it's a bone. He's feeding—no there's two . . . no it's *one*."

The bonefish feeds slowly this way and that. Now I can clearly see the distance between his dorsal and tail . . . it's a big fish. My pulse begins to race . . . it is happening, the old way, a reenactment.

"Lead him, John. Let him discover it. Drop it softly. Then hop it once," Bob says.

The fish is feeding toward me now. I crouch, make a sidearm backcast and shoot fifteen feet, sling forward and cast fifty feet.

The fly settles with a tiny splash twenty feet ahead of the fish. He stops feeding—alert now. I hop the fly once and he charges, pushing a dark, rolling bow wave toward the fly.

"He's on it! Lift!"

When I lift I feel good solid weight. The bonefish bolts at the unfamiliar resistance and dashes madly toward the mangrove fronds, then turns left, running so wildly down the flat that water rips up my fly line. The reel sings sweetly and smoothly, endlessly, and I watch backing melt away. I hold the rod high and listen, hoping there is enough, knowing that even if there isn't I am complete. The mangroves in these moments are gone, boat and guide gone. There is just the fish running toward the horizon.

He stops then and runs back at me and I reel wildly and pray that the mangrove seedlings will not entangle and break him off. When I tighten, he is there, running again, this time with shorter bursts. I can feel him tire now. I bring him quickly to the boat. Bob lifts the fish and it shines in the sun. Its creamy white belly overlaps his fingers.

"Over thirty inches. I'd say thirteen pounds," he says. I hold the bonefish, my best, for a long time, resting it, examining it, reviving it, watching it, still, there by my feet. Then it swims slowly away up the flat into the surface glare.

Tarpon

"The sport of fishing is in inverse ratio to the size of the tackle compared with the activity, strength, and weight of the fish," says A. W. Dimock in *The Book of the Tarpon*.

Bob eases the boat quietly into a long depression. "At this stage of the tide there are usually tarpon laid up here. We'll watch a while," Bob says as he poles slowly along a weed line toward the head of the depression. I am armed with a 12-weight that feels like a broomstick and a monofilament-core intermediate tarpon line that can make a beginner feel like Lefty Kreh casting across a parking lot. The fly is a Size 2/0 grizzly hackle with red and yellow saddles.

I recall then what Stu Apte said: "I haven't fished for anything but laid-up tarpon in fifteen years." Staking up all day is a sunlit imprisonment.

"I don't know why they like this spot. It just seems right to them. But only at dead high tide. There! Didja see that one roll there, John? Seventy feet, one o'clock. Put it on him!" Bob says with that tensive command urgency of the veteran Keys guide.

The fly turns over and lands where the dorsal and back appeared and disappeared. I retrieve with long strips, feeling the strike before it comes.

There are two kinds of tarpon strikes: the visual one that transfixes you in terror akin to stage fright, and the blind strike that simply rips your arms off. You experience the first when migratory tarpon come at you running the edge along a bank and you are staked up with the sun high and burning a hole in the water. Then the fish arrive in twos, threes, or fours, or in strings of ten to twenty fish, or as many as fifty to a hundred in a spread that looks like a broad array of semidark torpedos. At such times your knees turn to jelly and you try to recall the sequence of things that must be done quickly and smoothly, with the space closing rapidly between you and the oncoming mega herring.

These fish are travelers, up from Cuba or the coast of South America, and their miraculous arrival in the Keys each April and May turns tarpon hunters into feral animals. Since guide Jimmie Albright and Joe Brooks got this hunt rolling back in the 1940s and 1950s the idea has spread worldwide that the silver king is the top of the game on a fly. The permit gets the ink nowdays, but the antediluvian tarpon remains the main event for veterans. Now the flats from Islamorada to Key West are hounded each May and June by an armada of flats skiffs and eager tarpon hunters.

What makes this fish so enigmatic is its seasonal travels. Divers report schools of tarpon holding and traveling along the reefs of

Places

Belize, Costa Rica, the Yucatán, the Windward Islands, Cuba, and the coast of Venezuela. Despite Dimock's early escapades with tarpon on the west coast of Florida a century ago, we knew little about this greatest of all gamefish through the 1950s, except that the migration began in early spring and the fish moved through the Keys and Florida Bay and up the west coast of Florida. Boca Grande became the honey hole for the live-bait fishermen, and Homosassa Bay in the 1960s drew the world-record hunters. The latest fly-caught IGFA world record (202 pounds on 20-pound-test class tippet) was taken there in 2001.

The tarpon mysteries persisted until modern research began to unravel the fish's life history. This fish needs the land—more accurately, an interface between salt and fresh water—to survive. Its gills allow it to breathe under water like other fish, but it also has a lung, which allows it to survive in anaerobic water, where predators with gills cannot survive. The tarpon spawns in salt water and its fertilized eggs drift into oxygen-poor brackish water, where they mature in relative safety. These lagoon nurseries (the Everglades, the Zapata Swamp in Cuba, and the lagoons of the Venezuelan coast) are the life link of the tarpon. Tarpon daisy chaining we believe to be a spring mating-season ritual, and we search the flats for backs and dorsals breaking the surface where the fish tail-chase each other in a trancelike circle. Their ritual has become ours; their seasonal movements have become ours. We travel to intercept them on the surges of spring tides. We look for them moving or "laid up" in clear water, where we can see and cast the fly to eaters, happy, relaxed fish that turn suddenly on the fly and follow it and charge toward the boat and, at our feet, flare silverplate gills to suck the fly into their throat.

You learn, after blowing many fish, that you must subdue your impulse to strike; you must let the fish catch itself; you must wait, wait . . . let the fish turn with the fly, then haul hard with your line hand and strike with the rod sideways—once, twice, three times. Then, calmly, you must think: *Clear the line under your feet! Make a small ring with the forefinger and thumb of your line hand around the line so the line won't jump off the deck and wrap the reel! Now watch the fish! It's jumping now . . . bow the rod toward the fish!*

These commands will be yelled at you from the guide standing somewhere behind you in the skiff. Though they are blasted from nearby and in high C, they will be heard dimly, as an echo down a long tunnel.

Twenty feet away, one hundred pounds of tarpon will leap from clear four-foot-deep water ten or twenty feet into the sky. The fish radiates armor-plate silver into the sun and its head shakes violently and its gill covers rattle angrily. You feel diminished and scared. And the fight is just beginning.

Somewhere in your recesses you recall that tarpon have jumped into boats and seriously injured fishermen. Subliminally you recall that a tarpon was found dead in the water: hooked to the face of a fisherman. Another jumped into a boat and hit a photographer, knocking him unconscious into shark waters, where he was saved by the guide.

Dimock says that first run will be as long as a rifle shot—two hundred yards of leaping, tail-walking, somersaulting, and desperate sizzling runs. If the guide knows his business, he will advise you to let the fish run, bow the rod when it jumps, and then chase down on the fish when it slows and you reel to get line back onto the reel.

What he probably will *not* tell you is that you have initiated a test of wills that can test your manhood. And if you have hooked into that "it's the size of the fight in the dog" one-in-ten fish, you had better suck up your courage and prepare your heart.

Master angler and fly-world-record holder Billy Pate fought an over-six-foot tarpon for eight hours on a 12-weight rod. He won.

The ghostly aspect of these fights, which can last fifteen minutes or hours, is the psychological connection, through the line, between you and the fish. Suddenly you become aware that the fish, a thinking being, is *testing you*. You sense that it has discovered your fatigue and it is revived by that discovery. It fights harder; it rises and gulps air, recharging its oxygen levels for another charge down the flat and another twenty minutes of battle.

If you make the mistake of fighting the fish with your upper torso—arms, lats, pecs, shoulders, and back—you will lose, and the fish can sense that you are losing. The answer, Stu Apte discovered, is to fight with the large muscles of your legs while holding the rod butt in the hollow of your hip. The guide runs you up on the fish; you get your line back on the reel by running toward the bow of the skiff and reeling hard to keep the line tight. Then, at the bow, you back toward the transom, reeling, pulling the tarpon backward, turning it this way and then that so that at no instant can it rise and gulp air or gain a swimming advantage.

You feel the tarpon lose its psychological advantage, its will to fight. First it has the hammer, then it tires, then it gulps air and runs and jumps. You hope it will jump, for when it does it expends precious energy and you gain the advantage. When it runs or holds, it recovers, and you feel it gain strength. Then there is stalemate; then advantage to the fish; five minutes later you have the hammer. There are times, with that rare "fight-in-the-dog" fish, that you wish for a knot to fail, for a hook to pull free.

When it does not happen, you worry about your heart. This dead lifting, you have been told, is the the no-no that may kill you. "Legs, fight with your legs," you tell yourself. The fish senses a slow tipping of the balance during the "fight on the line," the end game near the boat, when the fish sees you near and you see it wallow and turn to the surface and you pull it backward and turn it over in exhaustion. Then, for the first time, when you can clearly see its herring mouth and celestial eye, you want to end things quickly. Near the boat your shadow melds into its shadow and when you touch the lip-gaffed plated head and release the fish, you both have made a capture.

A head and a long blue-green shape appear behind my fly.

"Strip, strip," Bob whispers.

The fish follows and follows, closing on the boat.

"Strip; keep it coming or he'll turn off."

Within a rod length of the boat the head suddenly enlarges as the gills flare and the fly disappears into the herring mouth to which I am transfixed. The tarpon turns.

"Strike him now!" Bob says in a half yell, half whisper, as though it is not quite time to break a spell. I pull hard backward on the line and strike sideways. The line stops suddenly and water sprays skyward and over the boat. A very large tarpon vaults head-over-tail beside the boat, its gill covers rattling. It runs ten feet and leaps again, this time straight up, and lashes its head from side to side trying to free the hook. I bow the rod tip, hopefully . . . scared . . . in the hands of fate.

In its third jump the tarpon tail-walks two hundred feet out, then thrashes along the surface, its head wagging viciously against the pressure of the line. It makes a short run again and is suddenly airborne, I bow, and the class tippet separates. The fish is gone.

"There are others here," Bob says with a calm that implies *Nothing you could have done about that one, chief.* I stand limp and shaken, considering my alternatives in the brief encounter.

Dimock had it right: "If Solomon had ever fished for tarpon he would have added the way of a tarpon in the water to that of an eagle in the air, a serpent on a rock, and the other things that were beyond his comprehension."

ON CAPE COD

I want to walk alone at sunrise along a Cape Cod beach and listen for the sound of stripers crashing bait. The sand will feel cool between my toes and the sandpipers will run with small, fastidious steps ahead of the waves as I approach. They are hunting for food where the ocean meets the land. I can read their delicate tracks in the sand before the waves wash in to erase them. I can turn and read mine as the sun raises her banners for the day. In the distance a harbor bell buoy dings, a long way off a foghorn sounds, and the earthy aroma of marshes drifts and mixes with the clean smell of salt.

A long way ahead terns dive into the surf, again and again. My pulse races now and I grip the rod tightly and begin to run toward the feeding place. There stripers crash in the surf, busting bunker against the curved sand beach. The bait tries to escape by throwing itself up onto the sand and the terns dive and snatch and the stripers thrust themselves landward into the wash to grab and then wriggle back to the incoming waves.

I cast a Deceiver hard into the wave wash where the black backs and white slab sides flash. I'm into one! He rushes into the surf and dogs his way up the beach line and I run to follow. In a few minutes he is at my feet, flopping on his side as the wave wash pushes him toward me. I lift him by his gill cover and hold him high into the sun. I remove the fly and release him quickly and chase the feeding stripers up the beach.

ON THE AMAZON

I was headed for the Amazon River to fish for peacock bass, which is not a bass at all but a cichlid, an equatorial fish that hides its young in its mouth. I called Lefty Kreh and inquired about killing peacock flies. "You won't need any flies larger than a 2/0, Johnny. Anything larger is too difficult to cast. I'll send you some of mine," he said.

I then tried artist Bill Elliott—cichlids had become the stars in his firmament. "I'm using 3/0 and 4/0 sheep patterns—I'll send some up; they're outcatching other streamers, bro, three to one," he said and then rambled on breathlessly for an hour describing the joys and heartbreaks of piarra and celestial Cichlidae.

When the Kreh flies arrived, they were tied on long-shank 2/0 hooks, with luxuriant fistfuls of neon blue, red, and yellow Flashabou. I had never seen anything like them. I held one in the bathtub. It moved languidly, radiating colors like a luminescent snake. That evening Larry Dahlberg added by phone the hemispheric insight that Amazon peacocks are suckers for chartreuse.

When they arrived, the Elliott flies emerged from their sleeves looking like alarmed, woolly torpedoes. They were large, ebullient, brash creations that would require a 10-weight with balls to cast. They would inhale water when retrieved; they would re-quire a backcast snap or the fly would cast like a waterlogged mitten. The hooks (3/0 and 4/0) were heavy and needle-sharp. To avoid prolonged suicide would require extraordinary care and power in the long Amazon casting.

I sat down to tie my own creations with newly designed 3/0 and 4/0 Gamakatsu hooks. What I wanted was a chartreuse Lefty's Deceiver with impressive body bulk, a fly that would look like large lunch but would wiggle like a mortally scared, wounded minnow in the water and yet be easy to cast. This would be push-ing the envelope of fly design and casting survival—working in extremis at the vise and on the world's largest river.

I was asking too much from one fly. The hooks were the heav-iest that I had ever used, or seen. Adding a six-inch-long hunk of charteuse saddle feathers would make the fly as easy to cast as a feather duster and it would, as Lefty had warned, "sink like an anvil in a swamp." I carefully lashed feathers, nicked myself on the alarmingly sharp hook and drew blood, and finally finished and held the fly up to examine its profile.

It had a Deceiver look, but it needed more body bulk and a head that would inspire predatorial rage. To the next fly I added a five-inch-long body of transcluent strands of light purple Krystal

Flash and a clear epoxy head. I finished the fly and held it up to the light to examine its light-gathering and emissive glow.

The fly reflected light the way morning sun sparkles on crystalline snow. When held up to my tying light, it shimmered with an inner glow. "Close, close," I whispered. "Missing googly eyes and it needs a crippled action."

I returned to the vise, chose a 3/0 hook, and tied the same fly. I added large black-on-silver paste-on eyes to the head. Then, using a nonslip mono loop to allow it to ride free, I tied a sixty-pound shock tippet to the eye of the hook. I dunked the fly in the bathtub and pulled. It swam straight through the water. Its feathers pulsed enticingly; but the streamer did not hesitate with that ineluctible crippled-minnow gimp that inspires predation.

I dug feverishly through my northern pike fly box and held up a red-and-white Dahlberg Diver, a fly that would be outlawed if the animal-rights folks witnessed its compulsive effects on Saskatchewan northerns. The fly had a sculpted, red deer-hair head, with atmospheric mouselike glass eyes, a white chin, and a four-inch-long, white rabbit-strip tail. All in all, it looked surprisingly saucy, alarmed, insouciant, even confident given its mission. I had witnessed its action in the water and the pike response. I picked a 2/0 straight-eyed hook and began cunning work sculpting deer hair to imitate Dahlberg's genius. Then I added blue Flashabou strands. I dunked the Diver in the tub and pulled: The fly wriggled from side to side through the water. When I stopped pulling, it lay there . . . pulsating. I gave it a slight tug . . . it moved like an energized red-and-white leech.

"There," I whispered.

The Volvo diesels in the ninety-foot Amazon Queen thrummed softly as the boat churned through the night toward another moorage on an Amazon River tributary, the Rio Alesandra.

The river the next morning moved silently under a gauzy blanket of fog. Howler monkeys groaned defiantly across the tree canopy and were answered by bands from afar, until the tropical rain forest rang with a resonant arboreal roar, the voice of Eden.

The boat eased gently around a bend as the sun levered its first shaft of glowing light through the mist to the river. Smooth, glistening pink shapes broke the surface, rolling, frolicking, and jumping as though discovering for the first time the joy of water and its infinite possibilities—freshwater porpoises. They frolicked innocently, yet unaware of their shrinking microcosm near an intruding industrial world as the boat slid through a quiet tree-hung lagoon and passed, like an apparition, away.

Habier, my guide, is one generation in civilization—a true surviving native, his father having left the rain forest to enter the population of 1.5 million people at Manaus, to abandon an aboriginal hunter-gatherer culture and enter the cash economy for the first time in perhaps a hundred generations of living naked in the rain forest.

About five feet tall, Habier is slight, wiry, and irrepressibly, smilingly happy in a way that only uncorrupted hunter-gatherer aboriginals who have not yet been crushed by poverty can be. He is extraordinarily intelligent in mechanical survival skills and fixes anything we break. He sleeps soundly each night on the hard benches in the air-conditioned forward compartment of the boat as we move to new fishing locations, the keel occasionally scraping the bottom as the captain and his spotlight-holding helper ease the two-hundred-ton stressed-teakwood boat through the uncharted channels of the Amazon and its tributaries.

In a quiet lagoon my companion Bob throttles down the eighty-horse Yamaha and we glide into a forest of ancient dead trees. My first cast of the 4/0 Deceiver, with Habier crouched at my right foot working the trolling motor on the casting deck of the

Maverick flats skiff, drops in the long backcast. As it comes forward it just clears his head by an inch and sails between the trees and hooks three feet to the left and hits the rear of a tree with a loud *thwock* that echoes across the lagoon and into the rain forest.

Habier has been through this before with gringos and he quickly hums the trolling motor around the tree, grabs and climbs upward with his toes gripping the warm, desiccated trunk, and reaches to retrieve the fly from a small cleft. Suddenly he leaps back, as a large toad hops from the small opening. There are deadly snakes in these forests, and they sun themselves in the pockets of dead trees. Habier climbs again and retrieves the fly.

He will do this for ten hours, pointing, whispering "peecock" now and then, and climbing to retrieve flies caught in the jungle of downed trees and drowned sentinels that stand like silent legions in the quiet lagoons. Only the swish of my deliberate, powerful backcasts and forward casts breaks the stillness, unless Magellan geese are surprised and honk defiantly as they beat away.

The casting is godawful. The 10-weight is powerful; I can feel it load nicely down into the butt with each long cast. The problem comes at the end of the casts: There's too much weight in the hook and bulk in the fly's dressing. I must overpower the stroke to keep the fly high enough to clear Habier's head on the backward and forward casts. But inertia hooks the fly left at the end of each cast. The accuracy is destroyed and accuracy is essential in fishing cover for peacocks. When retrieved, the fly pulses and wobbles, but its speed is too slow on a single-hand retrieve. I begin a two-hand retrieve, holding the rod under my right arm as I grab and pull with each hand, as fast as possible, missing the grab then achieving a nice rhythm as the day wears on and the new retrieve becomes second nature.

There is a problem with this retrieve. It is the only way to speed up the fly in its movement through the water, and peacocks will follow but not hit a slow-moving fly. The trouble begins with the retrieved line landing on the deck at my feet. No matter how I try, I cannot prevent the line from creeping under my feet—unless I use a stripping basket, which I do not have. On the next cast, and on every cast, the line is caught by my foot.

My response to this impossible situation is to scream with each cast: "Don't stand on your line! Don't stand on your line, dummy! Don't stand on your line, stupid!" Habier finds this galactically amusing. He has encountered obsessed fishermen, but never a self-deprecating, screaming loony.

The first peacock stops the fly savagely as I retrieve it past a dead tree. The fish charges suddenly and breaks the fifty-pound mono shock tippet as though it is spaghetti. This will take very heavy tackle. With great difficulty I tie on an eighty-pound shock and resume the heavy casting, which must not, and cannot, become metronomic. I am locked into the most demanding intensity that I have ever experienced in fly fishing, enmeshed in a personal vendetta against trees, brush, casting gymnastics and line manipulations, and enigmatic fish that on this day suffer from lockjaw.

Despite the difficult casting handicap, I can feel that glow of intuition and calm when I know that I am fishing well. There is no time to contemplate; this is all action, planning the next cast, judging the distance with that sense of distant touch that makes fly casting, and fishing, so mesmerizing and full of expectation. When the heavy fly lands just right, up a slot and tight to cover where the bank drops off into deep, dark water, I retrieve quickly before it can sink into branches. My arms feel alive; my eyes search the water for that fast-moving heavy shape charging behind the pulsating, crippled-looking fly . . .

"Peecock!" Habier shouts and the water boils in a toiletlike flush and the fish charges for a downed tree to the right of the slot. A big fish, he is in the branches before I can halt his rush. Then, before I can utter a warning, Habier peels off his shirt and dives into the piranha-infested water and I can see his blurry figure swimming and burrowing into the tree limbs eight feet below. A line of bubbles leaves the bank and trails under the boat. "Cayman!" Bob whispers.

We hold our breath. A minute passes and I can still see Habier working to free the fish. Then he surfaces, smiling, with a five-pound peacock held high. He hauls himself into the boat with the fish and poses for photos. He has done this before. He says, smilingly, "peecock."

After three, the lagoons become very quiet and calm. Two hundred yards away, across the glassy brown sheen, I can see something different on the water. It looks like a school of bubbles effervescing to the surface, as though someone had dropped large Alka Seltzer tablets into the lagoon. I point and Habier whispers "*peecocks*" and hurries the boat forward.

"At certain times in the late afternoons and evenings the female peacock releases her young from the protection of her mouth to swim free in the lagoon," Bob explains. "If you cast long across the school of young so your fly lands on the opposite side of it, then retrieve the fly back through the school, she will attack the fly. She thinks that it is attacking her young. This is a setup, a sure thing. Cast long and retrieve fast."

The cast sails over the effervescing bubbles and I pull with a hurried two-hand retrieve. There is a savage strike, I set up hard, and the line slices the water with a deep ripping sound as the huge female heads for deeper water. There is no turning or stopping her; she has her head, and her combined mass and strength are too much. I can only allow her to run—and fortunately she is running away from cover.

Then the hook pulls free. The fly comes sailing back to me and I am left with that emptiness of lost dreams, the feeling that only the lone fisherman or hunter can understand and share. The great peacock, which Habier estimated at fifteen pounds, was gone, but it has joined the live pool of searing events that I husband selfishly. The fly was mine. Tattered from combat, it is now retired in a box by my desk, a heroic memento.

IN LABRADOR

The DeHavilland Otter throbbed and shook and Marcel the pilot clutched the giant stick between his frail little arms as though life itself was about to be given its first—or last—launch. I could see nothing over the raised cowling. He advanced the throttle between us and lurched backward on the stick. The engine, which had started with deep-throated coughs, roared with a baritone blast. The metal airframe shuddered as the giant engine cleared its throat. Marcel gave it the gas and it roared smoothly and settled back and shot forward and down a lake of glasslike liquid amber and onto its pontoon step, and, magically, we were airborne.

Bush planes are the symbol of wilderness adventure, but not until you reach that moment of truth, skimming down the lake where the bush planes are all parked, do you actually believe the dream is about to happen. Whether your fantasies sent you into the tundra after caribou or the shimmering lakes of the trackless taiga after brook trout or ouananiche, here and at this moment you would, like Marcel, suck it up and depart. Behind is all that is known, safe, and banal, life's bead chain of obligations and duties; ahead lies the fulfillment of your dreams. Out there giant shovel-antlered caribou bulls joust head to head in tundra bogs and wolves harry the moving herds. A bull moose stands haunch-deep in a distant pond, its head dipped in still water, feeding. It lifts its head to chew and water sheets in shining rivulets from palmated antlers. Brook trout. Oh such brookies, finning and sipping at mayflies out there, waiting to fulfill a troll's ransom of dreams and memories.

Loitering in anticipation on the dock before the flight, the other sports and I had discussed those brookies. They would not be like our New England strains except in coloration. And they would be big. Just how large was a matter of some dispute. Their length would be perhaps five times that of a six-inch Green Mountain brookie and their weight perhaps tenfold.

I had called Lee Wulff for a description of the Minipi River system before departing. As a youth, I had been taken to his movies of the great Labrador wilderness and its giant brookies. At his home at Shushan, New York, I had absorbed his stories of taking two and three fish on a single cast, trout from four to seven pounds. Could the fishing still be that good? Thirty years had intervened.

Lee felt confident that world-class brookie fishing still existed on the Minipi. "Ray Cooper was a sergeant in the U.S. Air Force in World War II in Labrador who worked with me in setting up the military's recreational fishing camps in the Labrador wilderness. I convinced him that the only way to preserve the great trophy brook trout fishing was to require catch-and-release fishing. Otherwise, I said, the large fish would disappear the way they had in Quebec's trout fisheries. Quebec allowed its fishermen to kill the large fish, and they quickly disappeared from the province's lakes and streams. Once you lose the genetics represented by those large fish, you're left with smaller strains of fish. Ray's son, Jack, runs the Menonipi camps now, and he's carried on the catch-and-release regulations that his father began. The camps allow only one trophy fish per fisherman per week; the big fish are still there, from what I hear."

I discussed Lee's observations with Jerry Gibbs of *Outdoor Life* and Ed Zern of *Field & Stream* there on the floatplane dock at Deer Lake in Newfoundland. Bob, a stockbroker from New York on his way to camp for another fishing week, had new information.

"The last time I was up to Cooper's camps there was a fisheries researcher there from St. Johns College, Newfoundland. He and his assistants have been studying those great Menonipi trout to discover exactly why they average a pound larger coming out of winter than brookies on other Labrador lakes. His conclusions are not complete, but what he's learned is fascinating."

Bob said that the predator-prey relationship in the lakes is pike-brookie. In the lake, where the pike live with the brookies, there's a survival premium on size. The fish that quickly grow big and outgrow the bite size of the pike survive. Slow growers are eaten before they can outgrow the pike's mouth size. It's fascinating, isn't it . . . grow or die?

Jack Cooper had informed me that the July *Hexagenia* hatch was the one to meet on the Menonipi River lakes. A large mayfly, it sets the table for the bigger trout. Other hatches can bring good rises of fish, but nothing as reliably as the hex hatch, Jack said.

Labrador had been tortured geologically; you could see it clearly from the air. The great mile-thick Pleistocene glaciers had scraped and scoured their way south then retreated. They left behind a land of rock and water, with here and there a thin layer of sour soil where the trees clung, tentatively, to life. It was a world of green and blue, and if I never see Labrador again, it is the warm greens of earth and cobalt blues of sky and water that I will recall.

We landed on our lake of dreams, descending gently onto calm water like a goose cupping wings and skimming down on splayed webbed feet. When we stepped from the plane, it was into a magical quiet place. Waves lapped at the dock; sweet, clean boreal forest air scented by wildflowers and wild grasses washed our lungs; the lake shimmered in the morning sun, running away to its meeting with dark green spruces to the south and west. My eye searched its perfect mirror for the telltale sign of a dorsal or the gentle ring of a rise.

"The hatch comes just before dark; I'm Jack Cooper," a plump, quiet man said. "You've got time to rig your gear before the rise."

The compulsion to fish was too great with water so near, and we were rigged within minutes and sipping coffee on the dock when it happened. The first mayfly we had seen popped to the surface nearby. It rode with its wings upright for a while and then took wing. Another popped up and then another, until the lake surface quickly became a tiny mayfly sailboat regatta, extending up the lake as far as the eye could see. I imagined them, impelled by some natural signal on every Labrador lake, popping to the surface by the billions in God's great calling. And the dorsals would follow. This was it!

"Look at the Hexes," Bob exclaimed. "Keep your eyes open now. We could see a rise right here."

A gentle breeze had ruffled the water's surface so the sailboats rocked gently over each wavelet. Somewhere out about fifty yards a large black dorsal appeared briefly, disappeared, and then appeared again . . . and again, glimpsed, then anticipated and glimpsed again, moving randomly and not in the purposeful direction of a trout rising in an eddy line of drifting naturals on a river.

"Let's go! Where are the guides . . . where's Ray?" Bob demanded as he stuffed gear into his fly vest. The guides dashed to the boats and we departed, swiftly and in all directions, each heading for his own secret honey hole.

Ours was the Narrows, a slot between three headlands favored by the brookies during the *Hexagenia* hatch. When we anchored, Ray the guide slid the weight overboard gently and held his finger to his lips to caution against noises in the wooden cargo canoe.

I failed to notice them at first. My thoughts were feverishly on finding the right fly and tying on and testing knots. But after I'd had time to make things ready and quiet my nerves, my attention shifted to the water. They were coming. The magnificent natural engine that drives the Minipi-Menonipi trout system was shifting into high gear.

Nymphs were wiggling their way, in a watery coming of the hoard, from the lake bottom upward to the surface. Something had signaled them to abandon the mud six feet down to swim for the light overhead. They undulated their bodies springlike as they pointed their heads skyward and, in one multitudinous affirmation, emerged.

Peering over the side of the canoe into the clear, tea-colored water, I watched them swim, myriad silently thrusting *Hexagenia* wiggle-nymphs on their way toward an uncertain destiny. When each reached the surface, it popped its shuck and crawled on top of the husk, spread its wings, and floated for a while before taking wing. The small pops of a billion mayflies animated the evening hush, and we sat transfixed . . . listening . . . breathless . . . anticipating.

"There!" Ray whispered. A dorsal appeared, disappeared, and then reappeared.

"Lead him!"

I cast the fly to intercept the trout's train of rises, leading his line of gulping by about six feet. The Hex imitation popped over at the end of the cast, then settled gently to the water. I waited briefly and a head appeared, and then a dark dorsal, and the fly was gone and I lifted and felt a live weight. The trout charged away and down.

"Hold his head up or you'll lose him in the weeds," Ray said.

I felt the leader brush something and I lifted hard then and turned him up. He ran away to the end of the line before I could turn him and bring him back and lift him up for the guide to net. He was deep-bellied and his fins were edged in red and white, the red spots on his belly edged with blue halos. When I held him, his belly overflowed my fingers. I looked upon him as something transcendently important, a living thing of pantheistic beauty. He must have weighed five pounds. He seemed like ten. I freed him and exhaled.

If I had not taken another trout, it would have been enough. But there would be something else, a supernatural happening. It could not have occurred without a stroke of good fortune, my occupying the right place during a momentary nexus of natural conditions. I would witness what occurs in the wilderness only rarely, in civilized waters never.

The guide had anchored us at a flowage where the outflow of a lake gathered speed and began its run down a river channel to another lake below. The hatches that day had been sparse, so I had rigged a weighted Hare's Ear Nymph and was fishing blind for brookies feeding on drifting naturals funneled from the lake.

Things were going slowly. I paused in changing flies and glanced downriver and stared in disbelief and simply pointed. "There!"

Ray took one glance and jumped for the motor cord. About a hundred yards below us, in a side channel off the main flow, fish were in the air, very large fish, very large brook trout.

I had seen small brookies leap on small lakes and ponds, perhaps in pursuit of escaping *Chironomid*. Artists had portrayed them leaping after mayflies, too, but no one gave such license credence. I knew of no fishermen who had ever witnessed a leap-rising five-pound brook trout.

We were motoring fast toward the enchanted spot, and as we flew along the water, ahead I could see first one giant brookie clear the water and then another, as though for the first time revealing a joy that lay deep in their solemn souls.

"Drift down below and come up beside them by those alders," I said. The boat slid in quietly until it touched the alders and the guide grabbed them and tied in with the anchor rope. As he worked, a puff of wind blew giant gray mayfly spinners from the alders and gently deposited them on the water beside us. A natural drifted struggling on the surface for perhaps two feet when a large brook trout breached and, with a perfect three-foot controlled leap, arced up and descended upon the drifting mayfly. The fish was so close that had I grasped the net I could have captured it in midair.

The leap exceeded beauty. It defined the very limits of trout athletic prowess, spirit, and soul. To make it the brookie had to spot the insect from below, judge its drift time, launch, and time its leap to intercept the drifting insect on its (the fish's) descent to make the capture with its mouth. This is no small feat, comparable to a basketball player leaping to receive and dunk a forty-foot alley-oop pass. With one minor difference: The athlete does not leap from one medium to another—water to air— and back to complete his move.

I worked, with shaking fingers, to attach a Leadwing Coachman to the tippet. Another mayfly was blown, landed, and drifted. As I struggled with the fly, one eye on the drifting mayfly, the Leviathan of that place breached beside the boat and captured the hapless insect in a clean and nearly soundless and splashless dive.

As the female brookie topped her ascent, her eye, all-seeing and focused, fixed me. In that Snell's Circle of her gaze our souls were annealed. So it must be in such moments that the fisherman and the fish are one, for one cannot look into the eye of a great trout without seeing himself reflected there.

The fly was on, poorly knotted but so be it. I cast it and it landed softly just upstream of the boat. I watched it, fascinated, anticipating her appearance. She came. Up she went with her sides gleaming and that eye intent on the drifting fly below. And in that instant, with her so close and airborne, I hoped she would miss it. Her leap was perfect, though, and the fly disappeared with her. I lifted and felt connected as she ran. In a minute I had her by the boat, and then in my hands.

I wanted to examine her eye most of all, the left one especially, the one that had fixed me from the boat. It was clear, but now bulging, frightened. She was out of her element, mortal now. I examined the rest of her quickly. I held her gently in the water by the boat and released her. She swam slowly away. I can still see her.

STEELHEADING

The rain fell in sheets; then a wind roared upriver and drove the drops into our faces. Its chilling cold seeped into our necks and down our arms when we cast. We shivered and watched our lines drift and we led each drift with our rod tips and felt the flies tick bottom and waited for a tug. We gritted our teeth—steelheading.

Hal Janssen hunches intently on a rock ledge on the Gualala River, two miles upstream from the Pacific. He watches his line drift down the pool. Fish lie in the pool in suspended gray-green ranks, a steelhead military formation. Hal's line drifts slowly into it and his shoulders hunch intently. He whispers: "There, there . . . there." Then the line hesitates in its drift.

He lifts the rod tip smoothly, quickly, and the line tightens. A silver object shoots into the air and cartwheels again and again. It turns downriver then and heads for the ocean. It runs into the next pool, over the lip, past where Bill Schaadt stands fishing on his stepladder. It hooks left and is gone. Janssen stands viewing his empty reel spool. He blows on his hands and reels in. Schaadt bites a sandwich in his left hand and fishes a drift out with his right.

It takes a stolid steelheader's heart to meet the test of winter, from the Olympic Peninsula, to the Lower Peninsula of Michigan, to Lake Ontario. Ice clogs the guides, feet and hands have the same temperature as a snowball, beards and mustaches freeze, tippets cannot be retied without labored concentration, flies snag in the bottom, you must urinate, somehow. Your jaw is set, your knees ache with cold and resolution; your reel responds slowly; limp lines become cable; and your casts rattle through the guides. Your body labors and stifles under layers of clothing laid on like armament. Bad coffee tastes fine. Meat-and-cheese sandwiches delight the vegetarian. The world turns upside down; agony becomes pleasure. And you return again and again because in the gray depths just beyond your cold toes lie steelhead, a winter hope. They are wall trophies that pluck the fly softly and then run as though scalded. They dash away and leap into the sleet and rain. They will, with skillful fighting and good luck, come to you. They feel firm, cold, and slippery for a moment while you remove the hook. Then you watch them recover in the gray-green water for an instant and they disappear.

This seems surreal and yet it is a rush equal only to the first jumps of tarpon and Atlantic salmon or the first ripping dash of a ten-pound bonefish down a flat. And it takes so much technique to get it right. The rods must be just the right length and quickness, and they must have reserve power to carry long lines with long bellies to reach distant "buckets," where the steelhead lie in special, chosen seams of dark water.

Soft "noodle" rods are right for small-river Great Lakes steelheading, fishing different lines and leader rigs off the end of a rod tip, with tippets as light as two-pound test. The fishing techniques are totally different from the ones I used fishing shooting tapers on the Clearwater, the Grande Ronde, or the Skykomish. On these little rivers I'll be gently bottom-bouncing flies ten feet away with strike indicators and long leaders.

And in Michigan I must rethink my tackle, and techniques. I will fish in late winter for steelhead in their spawning area. If I suggested such a thing on a West Coast river, I'd be drummed out of Steelhead Heaven. It isn't done out there, for good reason, but it is done on the Pere Marquette, the Little Manistee, and other rivers, for good reason: It's the only shot fly fishers have at the Michigan steelhead.

~ ~ ~

"See that dark spot there by the boulder?" Jim Teeny asked.

I did not see it. I kept searching the riffle line that trailed off the boulder, my eye scanning up and down the interface of the fast and slow water. I knew what I was looking for. I'd trained my eye many years before on the Willoughby River in northern Vermont, searching for spring-run rainbows. The good fishermen spent 80 percent of their time searching for fish and 20 percent actually fishing. It had been the same on the Pere Marquette. You had to spot the fish first and then fish for them. Otherwise you were wasting your time.

But this was Jimmy's home water in Oregon. He knew where the steelhead would be. They had been hiding in the same places long before Jimmy first put a boot in the water as a boy. Each pocket, each run, had a certain bottom texture. And if that texture was just a little different than it had been the day before, then he knew there had to be a fish there.

As my eye became accustomed to the texture of that watery interface I call "the dark line," I began to sense the presence of another, smaller line. It was something like the sliver of gray made by a bonefish on a blue-green flat. But this was darker and with a special blue-black halo.

As I looked at it, the sliver seemed to waver with the dark line, but it had a solid look unlike the water itself.

"There! Yes. Now I see it, Jim."

And so it went up the river, stalking slowly and spotting fish where there had been no fish, and would be no fish without the help of eyes trained to see them.

Californian Dave Hickson has trained fish-hunting eyes like Teeny's. He has a special way to spot the fish in the water—especially the big fish. His advice is the best ever given on the subject: He employs the heart of the eye, or *cour d'oeil*, the eye of the hunter. He and Teeny, and all the great fly-fishing hunters have this eye; it spots fish where the average fisherman sees nothing. The eye perceives how a chameleon blends into his environment to survive.

Fishing with these hunters I discover that spotting fish takes work and days of onstream experience. It is the *suggestions of tex-*

ture that betray the large fish survivors—the six-year-old-plus fish, the objects of our desire.

And, I discover, being able to spot fish in one stream has application to all streams, and to the saltwater flats. To survive, fish must be able to hide. To fish to them, we must first know how and where to find them. Then we must know how to present the fly in a natural way, the way the fish expect to see food.

The moving windows are perhaps the most fascinating technique Hickson uses to locate trout holding deep in riffle water. The best way to practice the technique is to stand on a bridge over trout-stream riffle water and, with polarized glasses, first attempt to spot the windows in the riffles and then follow them with your eye, looking down through them to the bottom, where the fish are.

As your eye becomes accustomed to the moving pocket of flat water in the riffle and you search the green-blue bottom, you will pick out shapes that "don't fit." The window moves by and you look upstream for another to slide down to the spot where you spotted the strange shapes.

Your eye follows the window and then . . . there! The second glimpse is long enough in duration to confirm your suspicion: A very large trout lies down there beside that ledge or boulder. You wait for another window and reconfirm the fish's location, and this time you estimate its depth—about eight feet. Then you reconnoiter the bank to see where you can stand to present a fly to the fish. Your companion will remain on the bridge and advise you on your presentations—how close they are, whether to move upstream or down to improve them, whether the fish moves to examine the fly, when to strike.

This is fishing that raises my neck hackles with anticipation. And it lifts fly fishing to its highest levels. It is visual, sight fishing to large fish. And it is extremely demanding, physically and emotionally. You discover in sight fishing that you burn energy through your eyes. It's exhausting, and if you add to the eye work the intense fishing crouch that has become the hallmark of the hunting fly fisher, you have the makings of a late-afternoon mega ache, a backache combined with a headache. Your nervous system is ready to crash.

It's another winter, and there are new steelhead rivers to explore. Perhaps our icy paths will cross and we will share a moment—or not.

ALASKA

Catching a Pacific salmon grand slam (king, chum, sockeye, silver, and humpy) is one of fly fishing's lesser-known, and least attainable, holy grails. Lesser known because few of us have taken even one of the five Pacific salmon species on a fly, and most who have consider them to be dead fish swimming by the time they reach the headwaters of the Northwest rivers and the Great Lakes.

That makes the grand slam (taking all five species on a fly) a dream. And with the destruction of the North American rivers, there are few places in the world where a salmon grand slam *can even be attempted.* Still, there remains western Alaska, and especially Bristol Bay, the mother lode of Pacific salmon. It's possible to enter Heaven on these waters, because in summer pinks, chums, kings, and sockeyes run into the same or nearby rivers, and early-run silvers can provide a chance for a catch of all five species on one trip.

But there is a better goal. It's a cinch that if you catch all five salmon species, some of them will be logs, near the end of their run and approaching death. In some watersheds the runs overlap, but they are not simultaneous. Better to go for two or three of the salmon species near the salt, while they are fresh with sea lice still clinging to their sides. They are salmon that take you down into your backing and send you stumbling along rivers, dashing through a myriad of fish from seven in the morning until one the next morning. If you are one of those shuffling, half-crazed flyfishing troglodytes, you should depart from Alaska with sated eyes and sweetly aching arms. You will be convinced that you are no longer an epigone, a second-rate follower: You have joined the Tenth Legion. There just remains that one hyperion fish.

There are a number of camps and lodges *near the mouths* of the great salmon rivers of the Bristol Bay–Kuskokwim area that have all five salmon species passing their doorsteps each summer. The trick is to hit the rivers at just the right time—when the right salmon are just in from the salt water. They quickly turn color in the spawning rivers and their attention changes existentially, from moving and taking flies to regenerating their kind. The fresher the fish, the more savagely they take the fly.

Jim Teeny and I made plans to fish the Kanektok River, a tributary to Kuskokwim Bay on the edge of the great Yukon-Kuskokwim Delta. We would fish out of the Duncan camps on the lower river, fifteen miles up from tidewater. Our trip would begin on July 9, the tail of the king salmon run and during the arrival of the chums and sockeyes. There would still be fresh kings in the river, and we would have leopard rainbows and Dolly Varden as finger food. The salmon would be sea-bright and full of fight and suckers for the fly.

Fly fishers are tackle junkies. In our quiet, reclusive hours at home we hallucinate the dreaded breaking of a knot, or being spooled by a mythic fish. We obsessively, secretively, rig lines to probe the watery depths where no commercially made line can reach.

As my Alaska experience expanded, I had become increasingly paranoid about what I took for tackle and flies. I made special plans for this trip for giant kings and other strong salmon that seldom rise for the fly, and the right lines and rods headed my list of weapons. I had learned through sad experience that when fishing for Pacific salmon you must fish bottom or a life trip can turn into exercises in frustration or, worse, panhandling companions for spare parts.

I spent days scheming the line strategy and rigging—a complete 10-weight shooting-head system from two hundred grain to eight hundred grain, with the shooting line rigged with a whipped loop for fast changes. To that I added a Teeny line system, from T-200 to T-500. To complete my sinking-line system, I added Uniform Sink 8- and 10-weights and two sinking tips— one fast sinking, the other slow sinking. For fishing the surface, I included three weight-forward floating lines—two 8-weights and a 10-weight. Then I sat and carefully itemized the minimum line system I consider adequate for Alaska salmon fishing. I clucked "there" with self-satisfied approval. I tied and tested the backing-to-line and line-to-leader knots and clucked again.

King salmon are tough fish to beat on a fly rod. I estimated that I could survive with an 8-weight, four-piece travel rod for the chums, the rainbows, and the sockeyes, but I'd need a three-piece 10-weight for the kings, which would average around twenty pounds and might run as high as fifty. I knew I'd break at least one rod, so I took two 10-weights, an 8-weight, and a 5-weight for grayling.

I also obsessed about my flies, and when Carl Richards described his near-birth experience with a lemming hatch on the Good News River, I added a dozen mouse patterns to my Clouser Deep Minnows, Teeny Nymphs, Woolly Buggers, egg imitations, and Muddlers, all heavy-wire patterns except the mouse. I planned to fish on or near bottom 80 percent of the time.

Yes, I would need a quality reel with a good drag system and a minimum of two hundred yards of twenty-pound backing. I would still be taking a chance with a fifty-pound king. A reel that would take two hundred yards of thirty-pound backing and the fly line would be ideal. It could handle all the salmon, and particularly the kings. I included in my gear two lightweight salt-water reels (one with two hundred yards of thirty-pound backing and another with two hundred yards of twenty-pound) and a 5-weight trout reel for rainbows and grayling.

Places

—

125

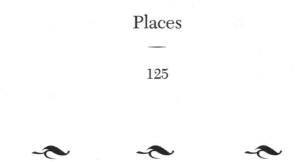

When you fly over the Kilbuck Mountains, heading west toward the Bering Sea on Alaska's western littoral, the mountains fall away and a lake plain rises like a green carpet dotted with sapphires to meet you. In a small plane you feel diminished by the sight, and as you approach the Yup'ik village of Bethel, you realize just how remote from civilization you are. Down there a Stanley Kubrick–style hospital sits like a large, partially squashed, metallic yellow banana amid a cluster of shanties. A lonely five miles of paved road runs through the village founded by Moravian missionaries in 1884. Its buildings are constructed on posts to survive the permafrost. It looks healthy but tentative and alone, perched there on the edge of one of the world's largest river deltas formed where the two-thousand-mile Yukon and the eight-hundred-mile Kuskokwim rivers become neighbors.

Life on the delta was always tenuous for hunter-gatherers, but the lake-filled plain is one of the world's great waterfowl nesting grounds, and the salmon runs of the two rivers made life possible for the Yup'iks, who believed that the earth was created, or scratched, by a great raven, who carved out the gorges of the

Yukon and Kuskokwim rivers, lakes, and streams with its talons. About ten thousand Yup'iks, the largest ethnic Native concentration in Alaska, inhabited the delta at the time of the arrival of white man in the 19th century. Today sixteen thousand people live in Bethel.

The Kanektok slides out of the Kilbuck Mountains, across the ancient Kuskokwim floodplain and into Kuskokwim Bay. Its graveled runs are spawning grounds for all five Pacific salmon species. One hundred fifty miles to the west lie Nunivak Island and the Bering Sea. The Duncans lease sport-fishing rights on the river from the Yup'iks of Quinhagak, the native village near the river's outflow into Kuskokwim Bay.

In late June and early July, when the kings are in the river and the chums and sockeye are arriving, the Kanektok buzzes with urgent, purposeful life. The natives pound up- and downriver in family boatloads, netting and drying fish for winter food in their summer camps. They pass boatloads of white sport fishermen in search of fish for fun.

And the river is so full of fish. The long holes near the tidewater hold great congregations of silver salmon, all preparing for the move upstream to spawn and die. The kings are a dominant presence. They appropriate the water they want, and the smaller chums, newly striped with watermarks, move aside for them. The sockeyes, slim and shining like highly polished torpedoes, lay up quietly in the sloughs and then swim upriver in great V-shaped wedges in the half-light of the Arctic summer nights. The fish are in and everyone is fishing, including the occasional bear, whose prints mark sandbars and whose scent turns the camp dog into a barking, schizophrenic canine.

There are so many fish and fishermen that you metamorphose into a round-the-clock predator, chasing them frantically until, exhausted, you drop. Then in a few brief hours you rise, eat, and go out again, hunting big, bright fish, fighting them passionately, searching for that obsessively imagined Great One. Sight fishing to Pacific salmon is an intense visual and emotional feast for excited nerve endings, like sight fishing to double-digit bonefish on an undisturbed ocean flat.

All the king salmon pools are within fifteen miles of camp, and where the salmon lie each year on their movements upriver is predictable unless the river floods in runoff and changes its familiar bottom geography.

You motor to the Ten Minute Hole and, as the guide drifts the boat through, you stand on the deck and search for the large rust-green shapes of the kings resting on their upriver migration.

You sight fish to the shapes as you stand on the sand-and-gravel banksides and cast the heavy lines upstream of the brown-green forms barely visible in the green-gray water. Casting the lines is relatively easy; casting them long requires skill. The twenty-seven-foot tapers built into running lines must be slung with a smooth, high delivery, the excess line held in your line hand as loops that shoot as the heavy taper pulls them up into the guides. The head must be the right weight of sinking line for the speed and depth of the water, for when the head hits the water it must sink quickly through the current so the fly reaches bottom as it approaches the fish. The fly must bounce or crawl across bottom or the king will not grab it.

If your eyesight is good, and you use high-quality polarized glasses, you can spot the movement of the fish's head when it takes the fly and the line goes tight and you lift.

The king may hesitate momentarily, not realizing that it is hooked, or it may charge off and into the air or simply turn and begin a long, unstoppable run downriver, quickly into your backing. You yell "Boat!" and the guide kicks the broad, shallow-draft jet sled off the bank and the two of you chase the king through the long riffle water and into the next pool. Hopefully, if the fish is not too large and oceanbound, the fight will be waged there.

With kings, as with tarpon, it's the size of the fight in the fish not the size of the fish in the fight.

When it is finally beached, the king will average about twenty pounds, but there are much larger shapes in the pools, and the shapes keep changing from day to day as newcomers arrive and depart for the upriver spawning gravel. When the shapes are of the brightest silver, and large as well, then the fishermen and guides become very excited: A large, bright king is the main event in this fly fishing.

Chum salmon come in two runs. The largest, the summer run (fish averaging seven pounds), arrives in early June and continues until mid-July when the fall fish (averaging eight pounds, with individuals up to fifteen pounds) arrive. In the long pools they occupy the same water as the kings, and when you fish for one, you fish for the other. And like the kings, the chums take flies fished on the bottom.

Chums are powerful fish for their size and when sea-bright they fight doggedly with vicious rolling and thrashing leaps. They take the same flies as the kings—brightly colored patterns (especially pink) tied on heavy wire. One day a green Teeny Nymph may work best, the next a pink deer-hair Polywog waked across the surface turns them giddy; then a black or red fly incites a suicidal grab. Which color today? Let's huddle and compare flies: only trial-and-success will tell.

The concentration required in this sight fishing is exhausting. Haig-Brown described it in *A River Never Sleeps* as fishing to the ripples made by moving schools of fish. In the Kanektok and some other Alaska rivers, when the water is low and clear, you spot holding fish and fish to them. It's like saltwater-flats fishing, except that you stand for long hours in one place working the fly carefully to one giant pod of fish. By noon your arms ache from maintaining a sustained predator's crouch, and the fatigue of standing and fighting fish extends down your back and into your legs. Line burns crease your fingers; your eyes ache, and your forearms are tight from strain.

The right presentations require the utmost effort and attention, but the hookups and the fights are pure avoirdupois— dogged heavy-tackle battles between brute fish and man. For relief, you turn your attention to the gentle side water where the sockeyes are laid up waiting for the light to fall to begin their runs upriver. You creep along the banks and watch the bright finning salmon in the deep aqua-green pools, knowing that tonight after supper you will fish for them on their migrations.

As the sun drops, the fish become more difficult to spot in the surface glare, so you fish carefully and instinctively to where they have been, and must still be. You fish urgently because the boat ride upriver for supper is approaching.

In the Arctic twilight, the sun slides slowly toward the horizon, and the salmon move. Below camp, where two flows converge, exhausted fishermen meet to fish the midnight run. Sockeyes ripple the surface in a long, slim back eddy. They are stacked in a little Grand Central Station of soft water, schools coming and going in a vast upstream evening push of fish. Jim Teeny waits for them and fishes a Nymph Tip line with concentration, the way a pointing bird dog approaches a holding pheasant. The line moves imperceptibly in its quiet drift amid the myriad sockeye, and he lifts and yells: "Fish on! Chromer!" In my half sleep half a mile upstream from Jim, I hear him exclaiming over another chrome-bright fish and I toss on clothes and stagger downriver to join the joyously atavistic hunt.

Some sockeyes leave the back eddy and, in schools, follow a leader over the four-inch-deep riffle bar. Standing at the head of the riffle, you can see them coming in a wedge-shaped ripple moving in the water's midnight surface glare. You cast with a sinking tip line, leading the wedge so the fly drops and intercepts the fish as they move upriver in the shallow water. The line hesitates ever so slightly and you lift and feel *fish*. A sockeye runs and jumps and jumps again and again.

You catch sockeyes there, with leopard rainbows and chums, until 1 A.M., until your arms and legs can stand no more. Only then, limp with the hunter's catch-sated fatigue, are your thoughts more on the cot in your tent than on fish. You must sleep. But . . . just one more tug.

The leopard rainbows are dry-fly light-rod candy in the rivers that drain to the Bering Sea. No one has explained why their markings are so brilliant. They are true river rainbows, not ocean-going steelhead. And they are suckers for the little lemmings, mice, and voles that inhabit the banks of their rivers and occasionally tumble in and struggle to swim.

Places

—

Under pewter skies, Brad Duncan sculls the boat driftboat-fashion downriver, holding while we drift-and-shoot the banks with mouse patterns. The water is cold, about fifty degrees, and the rainbows are sluggish and strike short. We adjust—leaving the fly, twitching it—and they take.

"When the water temperature rises five degrees, they'll take hard and you'll have thirty-fish days," Duncan says.

The river braids and in the side channels we walk and wade and work the alder sweepers, stalking the lemming hatch. When the rainbows come, they attack the fly, suddenly shooting out from under the brush, and are instantly airborne. After the large brutish salmon, they are luminous, like celestially marked rainbows leaping on dark Montana days.

～　　　～　　　～

The mind must slowly accept a return to civilization. The adjustment commences on the last day on the river, when you urgently search the holding runs for the largest king salmon you have ever seen. When the shape appears, unexpectedly where there had been no rust-colored apparition before, your stomach tightens and you peer hard at the image—disbelieving. It cannot be *that big*—one fish. Perhaps there are two there, side by side in a pair. No, no, it's one fish all right. But, God, it's got to be fifty pounds!

Wade close. Carefully. Get positioned just right, just downstream of the fish so you can hit the bucket, that sweet little slot in front of the fish's nose, with the first cast. Cast way upstream ahead of the fish so the fly will tick bottom as it approaches the shape. There! No, not quite right. Cast again. And again.

The minutes and casts string out. You are ready to resign—the ache in your arms and back is too much. One more cast.

There! *There!*

The head moves. The fly stops solidly. Then the bottom moves; the shape is under way. This weight comes from the center of the earth. Line peels off the reel. The fish runs away across the river. And then . . . Oh! leaps in a full-bodied, eye-level Atlantic salmon bravado.

"Is that your fish?" Roger yells. "He's big! Boat!"

We are in the boat and away . . . helplessly following. The fish leaps again; it drafts on the downstream currents backward into the lower end of the pool; it jumps again—it's a female! Then she turns and heads downriver. She will do what she will. There is no stopping her charge. We can only follow and regain backing when she—oh, please!—comes to rest with a pod of kings in the next pool.

Places

—

135

She *does* hesitate and I can put pressure on her, standing back from the shore with the rod bent double, the line stretched taut like piano wire. She dislikes the pressure and turns.

"Boat!"

Once she has her body into the current, the fight is all her way and we must follow—down into the next pool, and the next, and the next. She does not jump anymore. She knows now that something serious has begun—a fight for survival. I can gain line when she holds, but I cannot turn her head or move her body weight sideways. I'm irritating her, and when she holds in the current, I can sap her strength only by pulling her hard sideways. I must not give her rest. She must *feel* defeated before she *is* defeated. She can sense my fatigue through the line. I can feel her existential determination, and when she sulks and rests, I can almost feel her heart beat.

I know her life history—her mother dropping an egg into the gravel to which she is now headed to drop hers; the egg hatching in early spring; her tenuous wiggle emergence as a fragile swim-up fry; her gradual metamorphosis into a gaily colored smolt; her joining with others of her kind, the cloudlike young-of-the-year school that will drift its way downriver to the sea; her two- or three-year oceanic odyssey; and her urgent return to the square yard of clean gravel where this all began.

My odyssey as a fly fisher has taught me that the odds of her making it this far are in the millions to one. Now only I stand between her and her final genetic ritual, her grotesque physical deformation, and her death spasms in a quiet river side channel, where only a hungry bear may notice, inspect her briefly, and splash off in search of better fish to eat.

"You've got to beat her before she reaches those root wads. See them down there at the end of the pool?" Jimmy shouts. The fish is tired. I can feel her fatigue, and I can see that the shape flounders a little when I give her the butt and strain the line until it sings. Will the knots hold? She flounders back toward the current, and I lose twenty feet, then fifty more. She's going to make the root wads.

"Boat! Boat, *now!*" Jimmy yells. "Too late! She's gonna snag you! Boat!"

"Damn! Jim, she's in the wads."

In the boat, beside the wads, I can peer down and see the line and leader all tangled in the roots. Frustrated . . . desperate . . . I plunge into the water and pull and lift on the line.

"No! No! John, do it from in here, in the boat. We can free it!"

It's hopeless. The line will not come free. In a last, desperate, effort, I wrap the line around my hands and haul with all my might. It comes free from the top roots, but there are others. I haul hard again.

"No! You've got her! That's *her* down there. See!" Jim shouts.

Deep in the blue-green water, at the base of a root wad, lies a shape.

"That's her there, John. Lead her downstream. Don't let her have her head or she'll dash in and break you off. We can land her there, on that beach down below. See it? It's just right!"

I lead her gently downstream away from the wads. She swims sluggishly toward the large flat. Her weight is still so heavy that I can only watch line peel off the reel again. But this time she turns into the quiet water beside the flow, and as I tumble from the boat, I know that the end is very close. "Please don't let the knot break now," I whisper. "It's been an hour and a half and a mile of river. How long can monofilament and a 10-weight three piece last?" The truly large fish are usually lost with the leader at the tip-top.

Jim shouts staccato instructions. "She's tired. Get farther back on the beach! You can turn her now! Once she's turned, keep her coming. When she feels the stones on her belly, she'll bolt, so be careful she doesn't make a sudden move and break you off. If you get her far enough up on the gravel, she'll turn over on her side. Then she can't swim; we've got her. Keep backing up! Reel! Keep the pressure on her!"

She feels the pebbles on her belly, and she bolts in a weary, inertial-more-than-energy-driven dash for the main current. For the first time I can stop and turn her. She comes to me. She comes. The pebbles tickle her stomach, but she does not have the energy to turn and run. Her jaw slides up on the shallows and she tips on her side, and Jimmy and the guides and the other fishermen are with her. "There!"

I can touch her now for the first time. When I grasp the hard muscular wrist of her tail, my hand cannot completely encircle it. She is muscular, firm, full bellied, and cold in my hands. I can lift her only momentarily. She is the largest freshwater fish I have ever held. Her sides are already turning reddish brown. Her eye is a black onyx, celestial. As she revives in the current, I can feel her full strength . . . pulsing, reviving. Then I feel something tight within me release, as though a heavy stress had been lifted from my heart. I relax and exhale deeply.

She quivers anxiously; she needs to be off upriver. She is de-termined—strong again. It cannot be that she will spawn and quickly die. She seems immortal. I slowly, reluctantly, release my grip on her tail wrist. She senses freedom . . . and she charges away, sending rooster tails across the shallows as she heads for the main current.

She is gone. I have her here, still with me.

The Yup'iks believe that to fish for fun is a sin: Fishing must be for food. This is not sin. This is communion.

ON THE KULIK

The Kulik River is full of red sockeye salmon as we fly into camp. We can see them from the bush plane as we make the circle to land, banking above the river behind the camp. The sockeye are spaced evenly in the river, and they are dark red and make the blue water of the river look like a sinuous checkerboard.

We bank and come in fast and taxi up to the sand beach in front of the cabins set snugly against the south-facing hill on the north end of Nonvianek Lake. Behind the hill are mountain crags and rolling upland tundra. The air is autumn clear and the flinty crags and tundra valleys remind me of a Montana autumn. We are in the river of sockeyes an hour later.

On this September day the sockeyes lie spawning in the mile of river between Kulik and Nonvianek lakes. A million fish evenly spaced along the river in breeding schools. I watch them, fighting, dropping eggs, digging redds, angrily chasing competitors. The males, with their mouth parts hooking into a kype more and more each day, are fiercely beautiful.

I wade upstream through a river of blue, among thousands of red-backed, darting, thrashing, digging fish. When I approach, they flee in schools, then return quickly to their spawning and fighting. The males run at each other and thrash on the surface. In the backwaters, spent and dying sockeyes thrash and roll spasmodically. Dead sockeyes lie rotting along the shorelines, and fish stench overwhelms the air and water. Spawning and death spasms surround and immerse me. I feel taken down into the water by it and become part of the birth-death orgasm.

Fly fishing seems an effete act in such a setting, but I fish and immediately snag one of the thrashing sockeyes—*not* my quarry. I want the rainbows that lie obscured between the sockeyes, feeding on the eggs as they exude from the fecund females. The river runs full of spawn, a great milk shake fresh from a natural blender. The rainbows lie behind the sockeyes and dart through the spawners—gray destroyers slicing through a large convoy of heavy ships. The rainbows snap up the drifting eggs. The sockeyes chase them unsuccessfully; the rainbows are too fast. They are fat rainbows, much heavier than the swift-water 'bows I have known in the rivers of New England. These rainbows are egg-full, gorging themselves before the lean months of winter.

I can't get to the rainbows for the damned sockeyes. I'm fishing in a fisherman's paradise, but there are too many fish. I keep hooking the sockeyes on the swing. The rainbows are there, but the sockeyes are bigger and more numerous. I hook one, play it in after fifteen minutes of workhorse tug-of-war, and release it. I'm into the dorsal fin of another sockeye immediately. Finally, I rip the fly off and stomp to the bank to reconnoiter and regroup.

The still water at the bank sickens me. Rotting sockeyes pave the cobblestones. It's impossible to walk without stepping on— and into—rotting fish, fetid fish. When I step on the soft rotted flesh of a salmon lying in two feet of water, the mushy feeling shoots up my leg. I peer down through the water at the fish-turned-thing. It is covered with a fuzzlike decay. The sockeye's color has disappeared. The fuzz is tan-gray; it covers the entire body—eyes, fins, tail. The decaying fish defines decay, the rapid natural conversion of flesh to another form. I know that I will always see this fish when I hear or read of decay. It joins the sight of maggot masses squirming on a dead sheep's flanks in a hot summer New England pasture day in my pantheon of flesh-decay horrors.

The rocks in the still waters are covered with salmon pâté. Salmon rotted and transmuted into a smelly sockeye paste have turned the river into a putrid, greased-cobblestone horror. I slip and slide to the riverbank, certain that I will fall face-first into the rotting fish. I feel my face sinking into the soft fuzz of a rotting salmon, my hands grasping at pâté-covered rocks.

You do not sit on the banks of a sockeye spawning stream during these final days. Dead salmon, sockeye pâté, the intoxicating stench, and bear crap declare: "Fisherman, do not sit here!"

The bear defecation is especially disturbing—great piles of it here and there, filled with undigested salmon eggs. But the trodden-down grass is more disturbing, and the tracks strike terror in the most placid soul. Mammoth tracks in the mud along the banks are larger than you have ever seen tracks be. These tracks and their makers are the biggest damned things in your life; the makers have claws and huge teeth. They are brown bears with implacable stares and poor eyesight; they dislike other bears competing with them for fishing territories. You walk upright and look about the size of a small bear. Walking on the bear's path in the high grass will be very, very dangerous. I think of these things on the bank, trying to ponder how to catch rainbows. I decide to leave the riverbank where the bears travel for the safety of the river. The river is safer, yes, much safer than the tall grass where the bears travel and can't see you until you meet them face to face.

One guide who knows about the bears confirms that they cannot see well. They don't like humans, he says, but they don't fear them, except where humans are allowed to hunt them. Where they can be hunted, the bears will flee, trampling trees, shrubs, and flowers to leave the vicinity of humans and their guns. But here on Kulik no hunting is allowed, and the bears have no fear, which is more reason for fishermen to fear the unexpected encounter. With brown bears the unexpected is always to be avoided. The bear-expert guide taps his shoulder-holstered .44 magnum. "Necessary equipment around here," he says, and does not elaborate. Later I learn that he has been charged by a large brown bear at his camp on the river. He killed it with a lucky spinal-column shot—the only shot that could have stopped the animal before it was on him.

He is still nervous about the attack two days later. When I ask him about his stand with a pistol against the charging bear, he gives me stoic advice: "If you're going to carry one of these *pisto-las*, you'd better file the front sight blade down smooth. You'll only have time for one shot on a charging bear, and when you miss, he'll shove the pistol up your ass. It goes a lot easier if the sight blade's gone."

All the mealtime discussions from now on turn to bear stories. The bears are on the guests' and guides' minds subliminally—a presence that becomes oppressive as darkness falls along a river camp and you scurry to do things before nightfall. A bear roars a visceral, barrel-chested declaration. You realize as you open your sleeping bag in your tent that you are merely a naked intruder in the bear's land. Let it fish. Stay to the center of the river where you can see its approach. Give the bear its paths and high grass, where it will eat dying salmon and take long naps and blow satis-fied brown-bear sighs in the steamy grasses. Give it all that and stay away from its path.

The brown-bear-understanding guide says a bear will false-charge with its ears pricked. It will charge at you to within thirty yards and then stop for a better look. It may stand up on its hind legs and look at you then, and if it does, it will look like a curious boy trying to peer over a fence. If it drops its ears, look out!

Places

—

145

I wade back into the Kulik River after rainbows, through the salmon pâté and the floating dead fuzzies to the swift, deep runs where I know the rainbows will be.

I choose the head of a fast, dark run beside a cutbank and begin to work down through the heavy water. The wading is dangerous and my felt-soled waders continually break loose. I cast upstream toward the bank and mend upstream so the line will sink. I want the fly to tick the bottom and swing by me and rise. The rainbows will spot the rising egg pattern and dash to grab it before the current carries it away.

I watch the line where the orange sinking tip meets the yellow of the line belly, and I see the line jerk forward and feel the jolt of a hard strike in my arm and shoulder. There is a violent tugging on the line and rod, and a rainbow shoots out of the water, shakes, dances across the whitewater stretch below the cutbank, and disappears, running back and forth through the dashing red sockeyes.

When I have subdued but not finished it, I bring the bright rainbow up and hold it under its belly and release the fly from its jaw. I slide it back and forth in the water gently until its movements quicken. Suddenly the fish is gone.

Becoming a Fly Fisher

—

I hear a swishing sound behind and above me on the stream bank. Eight feet away a large brown bear peers at me, its ears pricked and its face showing the implacable stare that says: "There is nothing at the center of this world but me." I watch the ears as I back slowly into the current, away from the bank and the bear and into the ranks of spawning sockeyes. The stench of death is on the river, but I do not smell it.

Chapter Six

A. Hassall. 01.

The Throng of Shades

Whatever, it joined the throng of shades, touched and unseen, that haunt the angler—fish felt and lost, big ones that got away that are the subject of levity to nonanglers but of a deeper emotion to the angler himself.

Thomas McGuane,
"A Word Record Dinner"

"There he is. See the gray shape there by the tuft of grass?" the guide said.

"Okay. Yes! Got him. He's big. We're awfully close to him. Won't he spook?"

"No, he's nymphing. You can sneak a little closer. Ease down to the edge there and flip the nymph just upstream of him. Watch the fish. If he moves to the fly, lift and be ready for the surge. He'll head right out there for the main current. Don't lean on him; let the reel take the run."

I wanted to watch the trout for a long time. I wanted to be alone with him. I'd never had such an opportunity to watch a truly large, wild fish feeding in clear water. I wanted to watch him doing important things in private. I was beginning, as a fisherman, to understand that each trout has its own personality, perhaps even its own soul.

I observed the trout in fascination. He felt comfortable—I could see that. And it was important to me to see. He fed to his left, then to his right. He was a happy fish, with no worries. Trout have fundamental brains. Somewhere along the line I'd placed them just above a sparrow and well below a dog in intelligence. But it doesn't matter. The wild big ones are difficult to fool. In front of me lay a six- or seven-year-old trout—a survivor against very long odds.

The Throng of Shades

—

Having come so far, to New Zealand, I wanted to rest and just observe for a while. It was something I wanted to do by myself, away from other eyes except those of the fish. Life had become a high-speed run down a great white way of instant-gratification hamburger stands, pop music, and stocked trout. I wanted to connect with this wild fish, alone in a quiet, clean place.

I squatted perhaps thirty feet behind the bottom-feeding trout with the river running down to me from my right to left. The lie would mean a left-hand cast or a backhand right-hand cast. Either would be difficult but makeable.

I examined the lie further.

Where the trout lay close to the bank, grass and small shrubs overhung the water. A good cast would have to fall on the grass overhanging the lie. The leader would have to fall on the grass ends and then slip off onto the water, the nymph plinking down softly just ahead of the feeding trout and free-drifting down the feeding lane into the sweet spot in the hole where he took his food. The thought of it made me shiver. In my mind's eye I could see the cast landing lightly and the fish moving quickly ahead as it spotted the drifting nymph. I could almost feel the first throb of weight as I lifted.

But what if I blow the first cast and catch the grass or bush with the fly, I thought. *I'll blow the fish for sure. And then I might not see another fish, and we're seven miles back in the bush, and we must begin the return walk soon. This might actually be my last chance today!*

I knew I could make the cast, but in fact it was a damned short distance, too short for easy casting. The short casts don't load the rod, so the timing is all wrong and the motion is a flick instead of a cast. I had to let some line out below me to judge just how much I would need to cover the fish with only the tippet. If I flicked too much line, I'd line the fish and that would be the ball game.

I let some line out and watched it floating in the water and then eyeballed the distance to the trout. Feeding confidently. No problem. Wait a minute. Was he feeding less widely than before? Perhaps. He didn't seem to range quite so far to the left as when we'd first spotted him. What could be bothering him? He wasn't tense, but he did seem less liberal in his view of the world.

"Right you are. Now take him," the guide whispered from his crouched position behind me on the bank with my fishing partner.

"Give me a minute more. I'd like to look things over a bit," I whispered. "I don't want to blow this first cast."

The gray shape moved liquidly back and forth, definitely taking nymphs. I examined the fuzzy olive fly that the guide had offered and wondered if the wire would be heavy enough to handle the charge by such a large fish in heavy water. I checked my leader knots.

"Right?" the guide insisted.

"Okay. Okay. Just a second."

I would have to do it. I flicked the first cast out and over the fish. *Perfect!* I thought as the line landed behind the shape and the tippet and fly settled in a soft *plip* just ahead of it and perhaps a foot to the left.

I held my breath and watched the shape intently for any movement to its left. Instead, it moved right, perhaps to take a drifting nymph. I exhaled and let the cast drift by the shape and then picked it up and made another soft presentation. It, too, slid by the trout unmolested.

"What the hell?" I whispered without turning to the figures behind me.

"Try him a little closer," the guide offered.

This cast must land on the overhanging grass stems, I told myself, *but it must not catch them.* I stripped out two more feet of line to the length dragging below me in the current. I made no false cast but simply flicked the line up toward the trout. The nine-foot leader landed on the overhanging grass and slid gently off and onto the water, the last three feet of tippet and fly landing above the trout. The drift would be perfect, right down his pipe. I could not breathe. The cast drifted toward the large gray shape. I watched for a sudden movement forward or a head move to the left or right.

The shape did not move. I let the cast slide through and sat in the stones and watched the fish. Suddenly, before the drift was complete, the trout turned downstream toward me, tipped up, and poked his snout and his eye up through the surface and took something natural.

That eye: It fixed me in an all-seeing stare, and if the eyes are the windows of the soul, I looked briefly into his.

"Did you see that!" I exclaimed in a whisper to my companion. "He took off the surface! Why would he do that when he's been nymphing all along?"

I sat with my knees aching and the stones hurting my butt and thought about the trout and his perverse behavior and the silence of the two watching fishermen pressed against me with the urgency of required success. I had cast perfectly onto the hanging grass and dislodged some resting insect. When it fell to the water the trout had turned and taken it in a downstream surface rise.

I searched again for the gray shape.

Gone. "He's history," I said as I rose with aching knees. "What could I have done differently? When he poked his head through to take the natural off the surface, he looked right at me."

"Nothing, mate," the guide replied. He glanced at me and turned and hurried upriver beside the rushing green water, looking for the next trout.

"We're over our heads here," my companion offered tentatively. "These damned fish are too smart."

I glanced at my watch and turned to follow the guide. It was all slipping away. Perhaps there would be one more shot at a trout before my return to the United States the next day.

I saw it unexpectedly, almost a secret obscene shape glimpsed suddenly like a dark truth. We were stalking upstream, hunting for gray trout shapes in the liquid greenness, when a dark mass moved sinuously alongside a boulder and into my consciousness.

"What the hell! Look at that there by the rock," Jack said. "What a trout!"

"Eel," the guide whispered, without altering his stalk.

I watched the creature with open-mouthed amazement. It was like seeing my first snake emerge from under a rock, a supremely ugly thing appearing suddenly in a place of great beauty. The sluglike creature was an offense to my senses, which had been conditioned to the sleek silver shapes of Atlantic salmon, rainbow trout, and bonefish. Things in water are supposed to be wild, graceful, and cleanly cut. This creature was amorphous in shape; it undulated through the water like a giant leech.

Its presence obsessed me. What dark force had sent this obscene creature to swim the crystalline trout streams of the fly fisher's most favored land? How could it survive in such surroundings?—there were few fish in the New Zealand streams to sustain such a massive body weight. Perhaps, in a stroke of evolutionary fate, a means had inadvertently become an end. The presence of this super predator might well have controlled the number of trout. Could it be that good at killing trout?

The eel undulated sideways as it swam slowly upstream. I imagined it sliding up behind a sleeping trout, its undulations undetected by the fish's sensitive lateral line. The eel smelled the trout as it swam slowly upstream on the hunt through clean water. The smell had come as distinctly and meaningfully to the eel as the whiff of a moose carcass to a hunting grizzly bear. The eel, obeying ancient instincts, had followed the scent slowly, still unable to see the trout ahead in the current.

As the eel moved slowly forward, the scent became stronger, confirming its suspicions of food ahead. Its sinuations became slower and slower as the scent freshened, until just ahead it could barely glimpse a darker spot on the montage image of the stream bottom created by its poor eyesight.

By now the rich smell of prey had the eel's senses at full alert. It eased forward until its small head was just inches behind the trout tail. There it held as if to make a final, deliberative evaluation. Then its head moved slowly forward, waving in coincidence now with the current. Its hideous mouth opened, advanced, and closed suddenly around the tail of the trout. The stream erupted in violent thrashing.

The trout felt its tail grasped in a viselike grip and tried with a tail thrust to dash away from the painful grip from behind. It could not swim, however, because its tail was immobilized.

The water turned to froth where the giant trout struggled and attempted to roll off the eel's death grip. Its thrashing quickly became feeble under the great weight at its tail. And as its struggles weakened, the shape that held it from behind began the ugly business of turning the trout and swallowing it. Finally, just the tail of the trout protruded grotesquely from the eel's mouth, pulled now into a ghastly grimace by the vast mouthful. Only a bulge in the eel's shapeless form marked the passing of the paragon of shapes. The metamorphosis of beauty into ugliness was complete.

The eel's sense of smell is legendary. One angler tells of catching and releasing a trout and rubbing his hands on his waders to free them of fish slime. A little later, while in midstream casting to another trout, he feels a bump, bump at his thigh. He glances down into the face of a twenty-pound waterborne apparition and shrieks in terror as the thing chews on his waders. The fish smell on his waders had made him the prey.

In New Zealand I occasionally glanced behind me as I fished.

Chapter Seven

Feng Shui

My Japanese fishing companion last night tiptoed around our room organizing his chi. As I lay knitting up the raveled sleeve of care, he rose quietly and began rearranging gear and kit on the shelves beside his bed. Alarmed at first by strange noises in the dark Yucatán *talapas*, I lay listening to waves lapping the shore. A *tink-tink* here and a rustle there made me envision a hermit crab scuttling along the tile floor. Had a jungle python slithered into our haven? Was the cottage's pack rat exploring our gear?

As my eyes became accustomed to the gloom, I could vaguely see his figure moving from shelf to shelf as he carefully arranged the elements of his physical universe to balance its yin and yang. After an hour of careful shuffling and fiddling, he returned to his bed and within minutes snored softly.

I had seen him behave similarly elsewhere, on the bonefish flats. While stalking alone on a particularly long Bahamian flat I would look for his figure a way off and glimpse him, standing, fiddling with a fly or with his reel, and I would wonder: *So preoccupied: why doesn't he fish? He's missing the action.*

Only later did I realize that he was a true fly fisher, in the Oriental way. To him the organization of his universe was the management of Feng Shui that created the balance of life, a prerequisite to happiness. I realized then that he had found what all fly fishers seek—a balance between the yin and the yang, the worlds of thought and action. He had found what modern life makes so difficult for Westerners to achieve. We are the people of the yang—action is all. We have lost reflection and the quiet ordering of our universe—catching fish has become an all-consuming compulsion. We find our moments of yin only in a quiet retreat or onstream in those moments of delicious evening,

Feng Shui

—

when the whole body is one sense and delights through every pore. It is only in those moments that we hear the aeolian wind.

The fly fisher's Feng Shui retreat is his fly-tying room. Mine is situated on the south side of the house, away from the road, where I can create a quiet, clean, well-lighted sanctuary. The moments I will spend there will be alone. There are no piles of unanswered mail, no television, no dogs tail-wagging to be let out, no phones. I cannot hear music or the phone. The play-offs are a distant memory. My territorial compromises have been made, tacitly, with Herself.

In one corner is a well-stuffed recliner; in the other stands a five-shelf case holding leather-bound books with familiar titles: *Matching the Hatch*, *Idyl of the Split Bamboo*, *Trout Madness*, *Walden*, and *What the Trout Said*. I can almost reach them with my right hand. The books, the chair, and a reading light behind open my doorways to the yin of fly fishing.

Hours later, as sleet pelts the window, I will fold the book and move to my tying table near the window. A drafting table that I have inherited from my son has a white top that allows me to re-locate dropped hooks; its movable bottom ledge prevents clipped feathers and hair from falling to the floor; an attached refuse bag catches my clippings. Along the near wall I have carefully located Rubber Maid plastic boxes that seal completely so moths cannot penetrate the sanctum and eat my feathers. My chicken necks, the treasure trove of decades, are safe in a hand-carved Chinese camphor box that sits on my maple gun case across the room.

On the west wall I have hung: a shadow-boxed set of flies, including a Royal Wulff, a Jock Scott, a Stu Apte tarpon fly, a Lefty's Deceiver, and a Muddler Minnow. In the frame, to the left, are the U.S. postal stamps that commemorate the flies. Also on the wall is a color photo of President Jimmy Carter shaking my hand at Camp David in July 1980, a gift to each of the eight fly fishers who came at his request to teach him the skills of fly fishing. To its left, beside the gun cabinet, is a John Groth pen-and-ink illustration of Ernest Hemingway's head and shoulders and, below it, Groth's illustration of a Cape buffalo charging a hunter, with a remarque: "To a fellow Hemingway fan." Next to it is a Currier and Ives color print titled *Black Bass Spearing on the Restigouche*. On the east wall a ten-point white-tailed buck peers down at me—taken by my father in Township Twenty-Nine, Maine, and described in his book of *New York Times* columns, *Wood, Field, and Stream*.

My room and its contents are important—it is, in part, the core of my fly-fishing chi. On the table beside my reading chair

Feng Shui

---

sits a Julius Vom Hofe nickel-steel salmon reel and its finely finished Italian-leather case; a mule deer five-point horn drop I found in the Gila Wilderness in New Mexico years ago while bowhunting for elk rests beside it; an empty bottle of Old Overholt Straight Rye Whiskey peers down from the bookcase; a Valhalla Cannes priest with a split-bamboo shaft, a brass head, and a Portuguese-cork handle, all boxed in a walnut case with blue-velvet bottom, sits on a shelf behind my computer table; three brass gauges, mounted on a walnut panel, tell me the barometric pressure, the humidity, and the temperature; an elk-skin medicine bag, made for me by my friend Rene Harrop, hangs in my gun cabinet and fills the air with the sweet smell of wood smoke.

It is all here, together: my books, my gear, my memorabilia, my mementos, my photos, my fly-tying treasures, and my magical internet link to those other semi-esoteric, exclusive brothers who share my passions and arcane knowledge. It is my chi and mine alone, but in other houses, from here to Australia, others of my kind have created their dens of solitude. It is where they pursue the soul of fly fishing during winter's yin. When spring comes, they will emerge, and in the yang of summer they will hunt the earth for fish on a fly.

The values of fly fishing are the fly fisher's Feng Shui. And it is the writers who continue their dialogue with the past, perpetuating the anxiety of influence that instructs us in our search for certainties. Fly fishers are conservative men who go in search of immutable truths, and in shared values they find them. They are library builders, symbolists, collectors, worshipers of shamans, atavists in gentle search of prey. They find their fulfillment by rehearsing shared ancient values and rituals in places of great natural beauty.

Chapter Eight

The Mentors

It is late winter 1951 and the New York Sportsman Show is in full swing at the Grand Central Palace near Grand Central Station in downtown Manhattan. Baseball slugger Ted Williams steps to the casting pool with former heavyweight boxing champ Jack Sharkey. Williams uncorks a ninety-foot cast down the pool and Sharkey matches it. The two champions continue throwing line until a distance winner is declared and one show is over. Young boys watching this performance are indelibly impressed that fly casting requires the skills of the super athlete. This, they conclude, is a sport for especially capable and knowledgeable adults.

The Williams-Sharkey routine is followed by Jim Thorpe, who talks briefly and haltingly about his days on Mount Olympus and then is led away. Then a short, stocky man with very black hair mounts the stage and begins casting—forty feet, sixty, ninety, the entire fly line flies out of the rod tip with a dartlike loop. It is as though the line is a live extension of his arm and forefinger.

To the audience it appears as though Ellis Newman, the rod, and the line are one—the dancer and the dance are joined. He pauses, withdraws the tip section of the rod, and casts the entire line with the two remaining sections. Then he disjoints the second section and the crowd *oohs* as he again casts the entire line with smooth sweeps of his arm. Finally, he drops the butt section, grasps the line in one hand and hauls with the other and shoots sixty feet of line down the pool. Tumultuous, appreciative applause.

Newman is not done. He calls a sportswriter from nearby and has him stand fifty feet away with a cigarette in his mouth. Newman flicks the rod and the leader tippet plucks the cigarette from the man's lips. Newman flicks again and the tiny yellow yarn on the tippet snakes through the air, around the man's neck, and lands in his right pocket. The crowd roars its approval.

The Mentors

This is Ellis Newman, professional fly fisher and one of my early mentors. The demonstration is for show, but his skills have made him the Lefty Kreh of the 1950s. He is a shy man who can make fly casting seem athletically easy, as thrilling as Michael Jordan going to the air or sinking a last-second thirty-footer with nothing but net.

Newman typified a small group of men who—in the 1940s and 1950s—became professional mentors to boys, men, and women who, despite the advent of spin fishing, thirsted for fly fishing but who had no teacher to help them along the difficult path to fly fishing's elemental skill—casting.

To see these men perform inspired audiences who had never seen a fly fisher before. They influenced thousands of youths and adults to take up fly fishing as a recreational sport, and they became icons for a way of life and the values it represented. They stood at the center of the small social network of fly fishing. Together with other fly-fishing professionals, they comprised a unique generation that had not been seen before—a generation that is now disappearing. We are witnessing the slow twilight of the fly-fishing gods.

Who were they? Well, Al McClane (*The Practical Fly Fisherman*, 1953) was in his heyday, writing on fishing for *Field & Stream*. Lee

Wulff (*The Atlantic Salmon*, 1958) was making films on Labrador brookies and salmon, running fishing camps for wealthy sports, and writing—books and fly-fishing features—for the national outdoor magazines. Lefty Kreh (later to write *Fly Fishing in Salt Water*, 1974) was doing demos on trick shooting and casting at regional clubs and learning his writing trade from Joe Brooks, fishing editor for *Outdoor Life* (*Saltwater Fly Fishing*, 1950, and *The Complete Book of Fly Fishing*, 1958), succeeding Ray Bergman (*Trout*, 1938). Joan Salvato (Wulff) was competing with men in fly-casting competitions—and winning—and teaching her skills to whoever would listen. George Harvey, after creating the nation's first college course in fly fishing at Penn State University, was teaching an entire generation its arts and skills. These were the men and woman who made their livings—small ones—writing and teaching fly fishing. They are all gone now, except George, Lefty, and Joan.

But there was another group—the amateurs who would become fly-fishing mentors, and gods, as an adjunct to their professional careers, or by simply leaving them. The reclusive and somber Theodore Gordon had set the mold in the late nineteenth century, retiring for reasons of health to the Catskill streams where he fished, tied flies, wrote eloquently, and carried on a correspondence with his British mentor, F. M. Halford (*Dry*

Fly Fishing—Theory and Practice, 1889), the father of dry-fly fishing in England. Gordon's tying and fishing experimentations, and particularly his writings, endeared him as the Father of the Dry Fly in America. His willingness to break the umbilical cord of career and family made him the founding symbol of something more—the modern fly-fishing bum, a man whose lifestyle follows a less trodden path.

Stockbroker George M. L. LaBranche (*The Dry Fly & Fast Water* and *The Salmon & The Dry Fly*—1914 and 1924) got rich while he fly fished. He cautioned that expert instruction is essential to the dry-fly angler's ability to place the fly gently and accurately on the water. His instructions on the professional skill levels of fly fishing were inspirational—and unmatched until the Swisher and Richards work on dry-fly fishing in the 1970s.

Preston Jennings (*A Book of Trout Flies*, 1935) became the American Ronalds (*The Fly Fisher's Entomology*, 1836), the true father of modern American hatch matching, carefully researching and detailing the important aquatic insects and baitfish of the Eastern trout streams he fished. His seminal book inspired Schoharie River innkeeper Art Flick, who wrote the classic *Art Flick's Streamside Guide to Naturals and Their Imitations* (1947). Jennings, and a large dose of influence from the classic British angling writers, inspired Vincent C. Marinaro (A Modern Dry-Fly Code, 1950). The work of Ronalds, Jennings, Flick, and others also inspired Ernest G. Schwiebert Jr., an undergraduate at Ohio State University in the early 1950s, to write his classic Matching the Hatch (1955). And they inspired Doug Swisher and Dr. Carl Richards to research streams and their insects and write Selective Trout (1971) and Fly Fishing Strategy (1975) and twelve other books. Jennings's writings sent Al Caucci and Bob Nastasi into the Delaware River watershed streams to begin intensive amateur entomological research and to write Hatches (1975) and later Hatches II. And these works inspired Gary LaFontaine, the Ronalds of the Rockies, to write his massively researched Caddisflies (1983).

It is astounding to me that I have known or met many of these men, for many of them lived during my lifetime—and they all, personally or in their writings, became my mentors. That happy circumstance occurred because I lived during the six decades from 1940 through 2000, when the great advances in American entomology-based fly fishing occurred, most of it thanks to these men and their writings. It was also my good luck to be managing editor and then editor-publisher of Fly Fisherman magazine from 1978 through 2001—two-plus decades when fly fishing became a more broadly popular sport in the United States and across the world. Working with authors who personified, and created, the ideals of the sport gave me access to their writings, their fishing, and their inner feelings on fly fishing. Most of them became good friends.

Is there a common thread among these men? What is it that made, and makes, them tick? Did they create new knowledge? Obviously they were all hunters of fish—they wanted to catch them on a fly—but we must go to the inner man to discover his instincts, the chords that send him obsessively to the streams in search of . . . what?

It is important to understand that sport fishing, compared to fishing for survival, did not exist in North America until after the mid–nineteenth century. These men, the icons of fly fishing, introduced the sport from England and developed it on this continent. Why did they fish for sport? The answers are elemental yet complex—personal and social. Their writings—their values—are our values, their *Umwelten* has become our *Umwelten*, our world.

In considering the values of our mentors we should first consider our own values. What kind of fly fisher am I, and what do I want to become? The amateur entomologist is a phenomenon of our time, and I have, through reading their thoughts and fishing with them, absorbed their values. But as historian Paul Schullery has noted in his classic *American Fly Fishing* (1987), few anglers can (or want to) reach these levels of commitment. Most of us want recreation, sport, and relaxation onstream. Schullery quotes artist–fly fisher John Atherton on this subject:

> The fisherman who takes what sport he can find, who is not apt to devote much time to the collection of natural insects while on the stream and who prefers to let others do his research and experimentation is the man we most frequently meet with a flyrod. He may be allowed only a few weekends in the entire season, and he prefers to devote them to actual fishing rather than to the note-taking and close observation of the naturalist.

Atherton goes on to point out that for most anglers anything that involves work, other than wading or hiking to and from their car, should be avoided if their "fishing is for pure pleasure." He says, "As soon as sport becomes a pursuit, or resembles anything other than sport itself, it loses its main attraction."

Atherton describes me to a T. I'm no Thoreau in hiding. In my idle hours I read and absorb the wisdom of the Big Men of our sport, for they open the doors to higher understandings. They enlarge my universe, and they provide me with new horizons. Will I begin to carry a seine and a petrie dish onstream? Perhaps, someday when it is time to be old, when I must trim sail, when I have but one stream like Workman's Brook to call my own, when the small-insect hatches of spring have given way to those of autumn and the leaves are about to fall.

Our mentors fall naturally into two groups—the great generalists and the possessed naturalists. The generalists believe, with Atherton, that six or eight impressionistic dry-fly imitations are enough to match most hatches in North America. They believe that the angler-entomologists are over achievers who make too much of too little and that impressionism and presentation (of the fly) are king. Their motto is: Tie an imitation close enough in size, shape, and color and present it properly and you will catch trout.

The naturalists believe in this, too, but they also understand that searching out and identifying the natural insect in all its stages is key to understanding its imitation, and particularly the triggers that make trout take an imitation for a natural. The search and the discovery, with all the onstream and offstream work they entail, are the Golden Quest.

Watch the joy of Charlie Meck when spotting and identifying a fluttering mayfly or Al Caucci examining a petrie dish full of nymphs dislodged into a kick-net and you realize that fly-fishing fun and fulfillment is a house of many mansions: You can take its challenges as far as you want. My father had a question for Ernie Schwiebert Jr. years ago when discussing matching the hatch: "Why make something that is so much fun so difficult?" The answer to that question, of course, is that fly fishing is, in one way, like an onion: You can enjoy its outer skin, or you can peel it layer by layer, enjoying each as you go, but always looking forward to the discoveries and enjoyments that lie within. The peeling is half the fun.

Who is right? The past four decades have favored the naturalists, the fly fisher–entomologists, in part due to their strong influence through published works and in part due to their tone, implying that successful fly fishing requires more than mere mechanical abilities. In fact, the generalists (Atherton, Wulff, McClane, Brooks, Kreh, Fox, Harvey, Van Put) also believe in "matching the hatch." It's just that they are more relaxed about it; they look on hatch matching as an aid to fly selection, not as the sine qua non of fly fishing.

Here are a few of my mentors, men who stood at the social center of our sport. By understanding them, and listening to their messages, many of them unspoken, I have been taught many mysteries, but the real and fundamental mystery is this: nature itself and the ability to immerse myself in it with understanding.

LEE WULFF: THE ODYSSEY

Lee Wulff died on Sunday, April 28, 1991, at eighty-six, when his 1955 Piper Super Cub crashed into a hillside near Hancock, New York. He was flying with a flight instructor in a renewal procedure for his pilot's license when the crash occurred.

Lee was many things to many people: fly-fishing innovator, creator of the Wulff hair-wing flies, father of catch and release, Mr. Atlantic Salmon, designer of the original fly-fishing vest, book and magazine author, cinematographer, bush pilot explorer, salmon camp owner, and co-operator of fly-fishing schools on the Little Beaverkill. For all of those accomplishments he was revered by fishermen around the world. He was a mentor.

I first met him in the 1950s at his home in Shushan, New York. My father was the outdoor editor for *The New York Times* then, and he and Lee were good friends. Lee was making a film on Newfoundland, and a professional commentator was doing the voice-over in the Wulff home on the banks of the New York section of the Battenkill.

Lee explained his filmmaking and the adventures of living in Newfoundland and Labrador. To a boy of seventeen life seemed to offer unlimited possibilities, if he could just emulate Lee Wulff or some combination of Lee and John W. Randolph. Lee capped the tales of adventure with plane, camera, and fly rod by tying a Size 22 dry fly using just his hands and no tying vise. It would not be the last time I would see that done by Lee. It was a social trump card he played to great advantage with magazine and book editors. When the city boys witnessed such incredible dexterity, they were awed: They were convinced that Lee Wulff was the paragon of outdoorsmen.

And he was.

As time passed and I heard of or witnessed his accomplishments, I became convinced that he had all the elements we find in other men but also embodied other, rarer, qualities.

Lee Wulff was compulsively innovative. It was not enough for him to tie flies with just his hands; he was compelled to tie and experiment with patterns no one had ever tried or even considered. His letter of April 23, 1991, to me, five days before his death, contained a pike streamer with a detachable popping head. The piece he had written and enclosed was about needed changes in International Game Fishing Association (IGFA) record rules.

The fly was for me, and it was a typical Wulff creation—totally functional yet innovative and beautiful in a Wulff way. The sponge-rubber popper (adapted from saltwater billfish lure designs) would create a commotion on the water, and the four-inch red, white, and yellow streamer, tied behind a five-inch wire leader, would cause a savage predator such as a northern pike to attack. He had painted eyes on the black lacquered head of the fly to simulate a swimming baitfish.

In this fly, as in all his others, was the influence of Wulff the artist. He told me in an interview at his home in New Hampshire in 1973 that he had spent time with the Lost Generation in Paris after World War I pursuing art, and he considered himself first and foremost an artist. His movie awards were most important to him.

Lee was spiritually and physically restless and intrepid in the way Columbus, Daniel Boone, and John Muir were: He had a compulsive urge to explore and he had no fear of sailing out, or flying out, where no one had gone before. I assume that he inherited or learned his adventurous spirit from his mother, who had urged Lee to fish a stream near their home in Valdez, Alaska, when he could barely walk. Or it may have come from his father, who departed Brooklyn, New York, for the Alaska gold digs and later became a newspaper editor there when nothing turned up in the sluice box.

In the 1950s Lee flew his Piper J-3, the one in which he died, across Labrador in search of the great wilderness brook trout and salmon fisheries. He was the first person to fly a small non-military plane in Labrador. The plane was low in power and could carry little weight, so he always flew on the edge, in the danger zone where weight almost defeats plane. He flew in a wilderness where weather was notoriously bad for flying, and without navigational aids. And he usually flew alone. What drove Lee was the honey-hole lust that compels every true fisherman: the semi-religious belief that there are undiscovered spots where huge trout rise and he will stand there, alone, to see their dorsals and hear their sipping. If you have seen and heard a rise of trout in the hush of wilderness, you will understand what drove Lee to take such risks. He was the first human to fly fish those waters.

In an issue of the *Atlantic Salmon Journal* Lee described his airplane discovery of a huge pod of Atlantic salmon in the lake upper reaches of the River of Ponds in Newfoundland. The story was vintage Wulff. He flies over the lake and banks in a turn and spots a dark area in the water below. Something is wrong with the dark area. It is *moving*. A giant school of salmon! He sets the plane down and catches salmon at will—on every cast, probably in a place where no human had ever cast a fly.

In the 1950s my father was hunting deer at Dan Hartford's camp in Township Twenty-Nine in Maine with Bud Leavitt, longtime outdoor columnist for the *Bangor Daily News*. Lee knew where the hunters would be and just before dark Leavitt heard a plane. A little yellow Piper Super Cub dropped low and made a pass over the narrow woods road; something white dropped from it. The hunters picked it up and read the note wrapped around a rock: "Where should I land on the road? Put up rags on the posts so I can read the wind." While the hunters stood watching apprehensively, the plane landed. Wulff stepped out and said, "Will this plane be in the way, Dan?" Lee Wulff wasted no time considering his mortality.

Like other adventurers, he was restless. If he fished Boca Paila in the Yucatán with Joan, they fished all day, grabbed dinner, and then headed for the boca to fish long into the night. Wherever he fished, after the fishing he would often discuss fishing tactics and tie flies with the guides. He needed less sleep than the rest of us. He compromised little to age but limped due to a wading injury to his ankle. And in his fight with a sailfish on a dry fly, when he was eighty-five, he fought the fish sitting down, something he would not have done even at eighty.

His mind never failed him. In my last conversation with him, ten days before he died, he said he was worried about the game-fish record rules and wanted to do a story on it. He mentioned in passing that he'd taken the sailfish at Quepos on a dry fly and I urged him to include that in the story. He was excited about what he considered breaches of unworkable rules, but catching the sailfish was no more than a curiosity, something done—history. He was already thinking about other challenges, new places to go, fishing to explore with Joan and flies to tie or equipment to invent or improve.

The last time I fished with the Wulffs, Joan, Lee, and Nelson Bryant of *The New York Times* and I met on the Ste-Marguerite River near Quebec. We were told that new river regulations required that you cease fishing once you landed, and released, your first salmon. On the first morning Joan and I each caught grilse on our first cast and were done for the day. Lee was fishing a Size 28 fly tied ahead of a large Prefontaine tube fly rigged as an attractor. It was a special rig designed to catch a large salmon on a small fly.

Refusing to take a grilse, Lee repeatedly pulled the fly away from rising fish. Finally a salmon rose to the fly and was on. Lee played the fish gently for an hour, hoping the hook wire would not straighten before he could land the fish, which he estimated at around eighteen pounds.

Near the end of the fight, when the salmon was obviously tired and rolled at the end of a tight line, Lee remarked to Nelson: "I can feel him; I can feel his heart beat." A few moments later the hook pulled free and the salmon was free.

That night, in the cottage I shared with Lee, Joan, and Nelson, low conversation awakened me at 1 A.M. It was Lee in the adjoining room discussing how to tie certain Wulff salmon flies with the young guides.

In Lee the adventurous boy still lived at eighty-six. And in him there lived that rare sense of pathos that all true fly fishers carry with them wherever they may roam: that life and death hang by a thread, and we strain that thread to its limit in pursuit of what we love.

Having known Lee, I am a more perceptive human. When I spot a lone eagle soaring, I will think of him. He inoculated me with the protean urge to search out new waters where innocent wild fish look upward to their first glimpse of a fly. He represents the dawn, when the unsatisfied thoughts that all fly fishers have will be reborn with hope.

And when I am weary of the workaday world, and have worn out all my friends, I will go after a wild salmon. It must lie finning in a spring river where only the bush plane is occasionally heard and the wolf still harries the caribou. There I will cast a White Wulff across a slick of tea-colored water. I will lead the fly gently with the line so it dances on its hackles, making a slight V to mark its waking.

The fish's first coming will be exploratory, inquisitive, a deep swirl beneath the fly. Then, as it skims across the same place, the Wulff will disappear. I will not strike, for I have learned the lessons of the salmon rivers. When I lift, the salmon will feel that first unfamiliar tug on its jaw and it will leap to free itself. The buck will leap again, this time far out where the pale polished boulders are.

It will not take me long to land this fish, for I have learned from the professionals the value of strong tippets and the side pressure of the tarpon anglers. When I finally hold him in the shallows at my knees, he will still be fresh, ready to depart on urgent business. I will examine him carefully for net marks, sea lice, and hooking scars.

I will know him then, as a newborn of that river some four years ago, as a fry swimming in spring up from the egg nest where his mother had dropped him. I will know him as a parr with celestially colored flanks. I will know him as a smolt, changing bio-chemically, quickly, for his swift drift-swim down to the sea. I will swim with him up the Labrador Current to Greenland, where we will feast on capelin. Then, when the rotation of the earth is right and the sun begins to climb in spring, I will feel with him the earth's gravitational pull, and with him I will fol-low its magnetic lines, the ones that will lead me back to this river, to my own patch of gravel.

In his earth odyssey this salmon will feel no rock scrape his belly, no hook pierce his jaw, no hand hold him suspended in the shallows. I have, selfishly, deconstructed his fate to my own ends, but this is no sentimental experiment. I feel more like a citizen of the world, as though his natural history was my own. I can now rejoice that there are wild salmon, that they represent the wilderness that we have seen disappear, that they survive, barely; that as long as they are in these clean, lonely places, these re-maining rivers, there is hope for us—for me.

I realize then that I am in an ocean of subtle intelligences that surround me on all sides, the wolf, the chickadee, the caribou, the eagles. But here, from the vibrant salmon, I can *feel* them flow again into my hand and arm and heart. And no longer must I be—or feel—alone. This is a story I learned from Lee Wulff.

BILL SCHAADT: THE HUNT

If Bill Schaadt lived for anything it was to have his fly in the bucket when the bite was on. The "bucket," of course, is that sweet spot in a pool where the large anadromous fish lie. Every fisherman wants the bucket, but Bill Schaadt knew how to find and fish it better than any fly fisher who ever lived. He died at seventy-one on January 17, 1995, of cancer. The chronicle of his life is quite simple; the impact of the man on his peers was elemental, even mystical in the way that John Muir influenced those who knew him or read his descriptions of nature in the mountains.

Bill Schaadt was born and grew up in San Francisco and became a skilled high diver in his youth. He was a tall, swarthy, athletic man with large, powerful hands, a large nose, piercing black eyes, and tight curly black hair. His mien was noble; he loved animated talk; and his smile and laughter were infectious. He was a man among men, one who told his stories of fishing the way ancient respected elders told tales to eager listeners around campfires.

Schaadt moved to the Russian River in northern California when he was twenty and never looked back. He became a sign painter by trade, but at age forty, after discovering steelhead and salmon, and later striped bass, he quickly redefined his values and became the angling Daniel Boone of the North Coast rivers and bays, from San Francisco Bay to the Smith and Chetico rivers in southern Oregon. He became a fishing bum—more importantly a fly-fishing bum.

Of course he was no bum. Like the father of American dry-fly fishing, Theodore Gordon, he foresook traditional career and family ambitions (he never married). He pursued the taking of North Coast anadromous fish as both a mission and a passion, and that pursuit became the essential chord of his life. In the spots he haunted in search of fish his little fishing trailer became the talisman of fishing excellence that locals searched out, so much so that Schaadt often felt it necessary to hide it and his car from prying eyes.

He became legend to the fly fishers who haunted those waters. His casting skills were prodigious; his catching skills more so. He became fast friends with angling writer Ted Trueblood, who commented at one point that he'd learned more from Bill Schaadt than any other fisherman he'd ever met. Yet Schaadt never wrote a word on fishing except in his diaries, and, like Muir, he considered fame no more than a bauble.

He was a frugal, practical man, who gleefully and eagerly scrounged the cast-off "junk" of our society and repaired it to useful value. Thus, with his sign painting and his parking of cars at the North Coast's Bohemian Club, Schaadt eked out coin— enough to get him back to his rivers and his fish. Yet at his death he left fifty thousand dollars to be divided among the needy of his Russian River friends.

In four decades Schaadt became the most influential fly fisher on the North Coast. He is credited by many with creating successful fly-fishing techniques there for steelhead, king salmon, and striped bass.

A father figure to many aspiring anglers, Schaadt influenced the young artist Russell Chatham (*The Angler's Coast*, 1976), as much on life values as on fishing. Chatham considers him to be the best coastal fisherman who ever lived and certainly the man who caught the greatest number of steelhead.

But perhaps Schaadt's friend Bill Vergilio describes best the love and admiration that this man inspired:

I've read that a person is not gone until the last person who knew and loved him is also gone. Bill touched so many of us in so many ways that he is truly a legend. He certainly has had a great impact on our way of thinking and looking at life. When I say "out of it" or "in the bucket" or "lost motion," it's really Bill talking. He had such a unique way of looking at things. He would say things like, "You can have a million dollars, but you can't buy a strike!" or "Did you ever think that a fish never comes in contact with anything solid in its whole life until we drag it up on the beach?"

If it's true that "He is richest whose needs are fewest," then Bill was the richest person I ever met. He took delight in living on things he found or fixed and saw the value and significance of everything around him. Very little escaped his notice or his thoughts, and he placed each thing into the list of priorities by which he lived.

I met Bill Schaadt at the International Sportsman's Expo at San Mateo, California, the day the Americans beat the Russians to win the Olympic hockey final. Bill was describing his discovery of a large school of huge striped bass on the lower Russian River. As he spoke, softly at first, his large weathered hands gesticulated and he leaned his leathery face forward close to mine as if to impart a precious confidence.

He said he was riding his motor scooter along the river when he spotted something different about the water—he couldn't say just what. He drove perhaps another mile, then quickly retraced his way back to the suspicious water. "It was a dark spot where a dark spot should not have been. *A school of stripers!*" At that point in the telling Schaadt's voice began to rise, perhaps an octave, and his hands began to gain altitude. He looked deep into my eyes to detect the effect of this discovery upon me.

He continued. "I raced home, grabbed the rod and flies, returned and hid the scooter in the brush, and waded out toward those fish." As he spoke, Schaadt peered over his left shoulder and then his right to observe the effect on the crowd, now considerable, of fishermen around him.

"On my first cast the fly hit near one of those huge shadows and it broke from the school and charged the fly . . . a huge bow wave, a *submarine* following my fly!" Schaadt shrieked. He had lost himself to the memory and was reliving it as virtual reality.

"He took!"

All activity halted in the nearby booths of the fishing show. Along the casting pool people turned and then, as if drawn to the Pied Piper of Fishing, gathered to hear the story.

Schaadt caught the huge striper, his largest, perhaps in the sixty-pound range, or perhaps higher, just as a crowd roar swept the show area. The Americans had just scored the winning goal against the Russians. The hockey win was fine, but only a minor distraction from Bill Schaadt's story. He held us spellbound, transported into his world, sharing with him the moment that all fishermen pursue.

With Hal Janssen I fished a pool on the Gualala River with Bill in 1981. I watched him closely, as a baseball player would study Babe Ruth in the batting cage. His casting was motion poetry, smooth and effortless, a reflection of his life. In the last two months of it he remarked to Bob Nauheim: "I can't believe I've had so much fun." At the end he was still in the bucket, the San Francisco boy who had achieved the grace of fly fishing's Tenth Level.

Schaadt became a lodestar by which I set my compass. Watching him fish, I learned to waste no motion, to fish my fly in the water, to rise and fish before dawn and quit after dark, to fish few flies, to concentrate for twelve hours, to isolate and distill my concentration—to *hunt*.

GEORGE HARVEY: MICRO-DRAG ON FLAT WATER

It is August. The sun has just come up. The cows are beginning to wander slowly back down to Spruce Creek from their milking, halting in midstream for a contented drink and then heaving their motherly bulks up the bank to feed in the meadow grasses. Purple martins sit waiting on the electric wires over the stream. They fidget, preening their blue-black feathers, or flit out for a brief circle over the stream or a climb and an elegant knifing turn or dive. Then they join the others on the wire and fidget nervously. Bird anticipation reminds me of trout-feeding anxiousness—fish and birds go up on their fins or wings—watching. Down on the creek the water slides gently around corners, shining in light-shot, steamy mist. The limestone spring creek is perfect. Its inherent logic is a revelation about to unfold. It slides, indolently, toward the Little Juniata, the Susquehanna, the Chesapeake Bay, and the Atlantic. A rise dimples the surface. Riseforms send rings outward here and there creating a river of anticipation that somehow relates life to eternity.

George Harvey, athletic and quick at seventy-three, is on his way, leaving dark prints in the dew as he stalks up the bank. The martins depart, purposefully. On the wing, they make urgent *quick-quicks*. They are hunting now.

George motions urgently for me to come to him. Where he stands beside the stream the sun has entered to create a hallway of gauzy light in the chill morning valley. In the air above the water a luminous ball of insects dances. Tiny wings beating in a mating swarm make the sound of gases effervescing. The ball rises then descends, then rises again, sometimes holding altitude, then moving unpredictably again over the stream.

Below the swarm the trout are on the fin, patrolling at the surface in the riffle beside an ancient tree trunk. I wonder if they can actually see the tiny airborne mayfly spinners that they seem to sense above them.

George makes a swipe at the swarm with a fine-mesh net on a pole, withdraws it, and makes an examination. The martins pirouette and grab, black darting hunters in the white, backlit swarm.

"Look at this, Jawn. These black-bodied ones are the male *Tricorythodes* and the green-bodied ones are the females. In the swarm the males are on the top and the females below. See how they are all male at the top of the net and female at the bottom?"

"Get in there and catch those trout, Jawn. Cast right in there by the log."

It is not easy. The trout are slashing in abandon at the tiny flies dropping to the surface to lay their eggs in the little riffle. I have begun with George's green-bodied spinner, and I cast with quick short wrist-flicks. The trout sip the little naturals in the irised foam. I lift reflexively, not sure exactly whether the strike is to my fly or to the real things.

The trout and the birds and I increase our frenzy. On every third cast I hook a fish, all rainbows, each from twelve to sixteen inches long. In half an hour it is over, and we run for the car and speed downriver to find another hatching and feeding place in the warm, hazy meadow. When we find it, we cast feverishly to take as many fish as possible before it is over. Then the hatch ends and we recline on the bank in the shade of a willow with the cows nearby vacantly noshing their cuds. We discuss the black-bodied male trico and his green-bodied female mate and the flies that match them. George observes that he never sees the duns emerge and does not know when they do, but it must be at night when no one can see them. "The spinner fall is all we have," he says. "But it's enough on mornings like this." I agree.

Harvey, the longtime Angling Professor at Penn State University, does not fish with you—he *observes you* and *teaches you*. That morning Harvey teaches me his eternal lesson—accurate presentations made without micro-drag on flat water to discriminating trout. "Flick your wrist, Jawn. Overpower the cast slightly; then when the cast has turned over, lower your casting hand. If your leader is constructed properly, you will, by dropping your hand, relieve the drag that is imperceptible to the eye."

The results on my catch rate are startling. It is as though the door to Dry-Fly Heaven has opened—and the opening is *so simple*, when the mentor is there at my elbow, whispering wisdom on his river. It is as though the vague shadow that had separated me from the trout had evaporated and they were now *mine*.

George Anderson: Rifle Shots at Tortugas

Angry Crow Indian bucks had been shooting at the fishermen near Two Leggins take-out on the Big Horn River in Montana. The tribe had lost its U.S. Supreme Court fight to close the river to whites. The river quarrel had simmered all during that 1981 summer in the uncertainty of the FBI's efforts to halt the firing. George Anderson and I had decided to risk the fishing. He would introduce me to the river that had been legally closed for a decade while the court battles raged.

Anderson launched his McKenzie dory and threw himself into the oars, hauling hard repeatedly until the boat came up as though on step and a small wake formed behind. He pulled for ten minutes and then eased into the edge of an eddy.

A chill clarity hung over the river like October truth. In the stillness below the wheated bluffs pheasants cackled and the occasional bird sailed from the heights to the river bottom where the cottonwoods shone like Aztec gold. In the pool, along the edges of weed, large black snouts and heads bobbed in the surface.

Anderson withdrew a 5-weight and stepped slowly toward the end of the feeding line of trout. He stopped twenty-five feet short of the first snout. He flicked his first cast forward; there was a splash and he pulled the fish toward the stream center, away from the feeding string of fish along the weed line. He played the nineteen-inch brown to hand; released it; stepped forward; flicked another cast; hooked the next fish in the line; played it away from the others and landed it. He worked his way methodically upcurrent, knocking off trout at will until a hooked fish bolted upstream and frightened the remaining feeding line.

It was my first introduction to the Anderson techniques, which would astound me and later earn Anderson a reputation as the Rocky Mountain trout version of the Grim Reaper, or the "River Rhino."

When I tried his technique—what became known in later years as "fishing to heads"—I failed, but not miserably. Anderson hit the head, overlapping the tippet lightly on the trout's snout, on the first cast. I, on the other hand, required two or three casts to hit the target. And that, buckeroos and buckerettes, makes all the difference. I practiced what Anderson calls, without condescension, "the shotgun approach." He practiced the rifle shot.

It is a firmly held suspicion among amateur, and even veteran, fly fishers that highly efficient angling turns on certain stunts. Nothing, I learned, could be further from the truth. It turns, I found, on the practice of accuracy and, as one efficient fly fisher has noted, the "elimination of variables."

Great fly fishers *get close to their prey*; then they cast accurately, on the *first cast*. They cast to "a happy fish." Miss that first cast and you cast to "an uneasy fish." This simple little fishing nostrum separates the men from the boys. For these fishermen there is no rummaging through fly boxes to find the magic fly—just lining things up and presenting the fly the fish is looking for, *bang,* right down his pipe—on the first pitch.

Easier said than done. When I fish with Anderson I learn, quickly, to run from fish to fish. Line um up; knock um off; jump in the boat; scull to another pod and do the same. In an afternoon Montana wind, especially quartering, this jockstrapping can be a challenge.

Anderson's answer is to use a nine-foot leader with a stiff Amnesia butt and a relatively short, soft tippet. He punches the fly into the wind with a sharp wrist-flick, driving it down to the water so the butt lands behind the trout and the tippet turns the fly sharply over, straight to the target. The Size 18 dry lands with a tiny *plip*, a slight indentation in the surface film just ahead of the trout's snout. If the trout is hog-wallowing, with its snout lifting and falling above the surface film as it takes naturals in an eddy line, the tippet will draw the fly into the snout as the line behind the trout is drawn downstream.

Sound simple? It is, until you try it. To succeed, try casting into a coffee cup with a wind blowing before you take on this unique "game of nods."

I thought I had it all down pat. Then one evening fishing the Boulder River I located a nice brown randomly garbage feeding. Mezmerized, as any easterner would be with such a find, I spent half an hour metronoming my casts. Meanwhile Anderson dashed upriver from pool to pool, knocking off tortugas while I obssessed with one. His "run um down and catch um" pool-hopping technique, I learned later, was a favorite of Art Flick back in the 1950s.

Given the right circumstances, the efficient hunter of fish can conduct a slaughter. Of course this can become a numbers game, what many fly fishers abhor, for they lose that glimpse of eternity that involves a sense of time standing still and the refractive, kaleidoscopic beauty of place. Nevertheless, the feeling of omnipotence, of control over the fishes, can be irresistible.

JEFF BLOOD: STEELHEAD IN A BATHTUB

In fall, when the steelhead return from the Great Lakes to the land, the fever of big fish in small places is gripping. Standing in the Oak Orchard tailwater when the five- to thirty-pound browns come in to spawn in a foot of clear water can stimulate instincts long dormant since the Roman Colosseum. One has the urge to dash from giant fish to giant fish like a child unleashed in a candy store. The urge to catch lives disturbingly close to the urge to slaughter. Maintaining sportsmanlike conduct, where huge fish can easily be seen, and more easily foul-hooked, submits the traditional small-trout angler to pressures that he has never experienced before. He must have nerves of steel to follow ethical restraints that his fly-fishing forebears adopted over centuries—while catching dinks.

The modern condition makes ethics difficult. The fishery is man-made, a "put-grow-and-take" operation in which a myriad of nonnative steelhead smolts are released into lake tributaries. The fish imprint on the stream, swim down to the lake, grow large there feeding on bait, then return as behemoths to the trickles where they were released. When they are "home," there may be as many as two hundred five- to eighteen-pound steelhead in a pool the size of a resort swimming pool. And the fishermen, spinning to the left and to the right, may be chumming them (surreptitiously and illegally) or snagging ("lifting") and killing them.

In this setting fly fisher Jeff Blood (the Blood Dot fly) has emerged as king. He has hooked as many as one hundred steelhead in a day and released all of them, either by hand or by long line. I arranged to have him fish *mano a mano* with traditional streamer-fly fisherman Jim Teeny on the Cattaraugus River southwest of Buffalo, New York, just to see what two efficient predators could do fishing the same pool using different flies and unrelated techniques.

Blood fishes a Size 18 egg imitation that is deadly on steelhead. He fishes the single fly below a strike indicator, using a micro-shot pinched on a four- or six-pound tippet. The takes are subtle, a slight hesitation of the indicator in its drift, or no hesitation at all, in which case in clear water Blood watches the head and the mouth of the fish for a taking motion. Using such small hooks and light tippets, he will break off more than half the fish he hooks. His vertical presentation using the strike indicator allows him to thread the fly through the ranks of fish. Nevertheless, he occasionally foul-hooks a steelhead, which he simply breaks off.

Teeny, on the other hand, fishes his Teeny Nymphs in the traditional down-and-across presentation. With such stacking of cordwood in the pool, he must carefully mend, and mend again, a nymph tip line down toward the pool's tailout, where many steelhead lie. In clear water he can observe the take and Teeny claims, with evidence, that if he can spot a steelhead, he can catch it.

To watch Jeff Blood fish a Lake Erie steelhead tributary is like watching a cleaner at his work. He intends to catch all the steelhead in a pool and he presents the fly to them carefully and with precision. He often hooks up, fairly—in the fish's mouth—on every cast. He plays them quickly, breaking off or releasing "green" fish. His ethics are impeccable, tailored to the modern stream-full-of-trophies condition. He is a catching machine, observed furtively and jealously by others nearby. Hooking and releasing is his tireless game.

Teeny, the West Coast steelhead Doctor Catch, fishes with shooting heads. His horizontal presentation puts the fly in the fish's face—on some days his Teeny Natural is the fly the fish prefer and on others it's Insect Green, or the Egg-Sucking Leech. On Blood's water Blood is the top hand, with Teeny catching nearly as many steelhead on some days and fewer on others. Both men have found ways to fish morally in an amoral world of numbers— but they both count their fish. Each reveals to me his ways of fishing where the big boys in from the lakes fill the streams. It is Great Lakes steelheading, sight fishing to silver torpedoes.

Here, as in Michigan's Little Manistee and Pere Marquette rivers, the steelhead *know*; they feel their vulnerability in the tiny places where skinny, clear water leaves no place to hide from the men standing near them. The steelhead answer on the Little Manistee, learned over the past three decades, is to hide under snags and brush. Peek into a steelhead hotel and you'll find no vacancy. Spawning will begin at dusk and continue through the night.

On the Cat a gray November dawn shrouds the Erie lake plains. The river is milky from recent rains—sight fishing will be out. Cabbages, left by the reservation Indians, dot the frozen fields.

The Mentors

—

Bent over like mummies in fleece jackets, we grunt as we tie on Korkers and trudge down icy banks to a morose river winding beneath laminar shale banks. The pool is two hundred feet long and narrow, shaped like a cigar. Its water runs quietly and smoothly through polished shale tubs. There is no sign of fish anywhere.

Jeff Blood takes the far bank and Teeny the near. They begin work. "Fish on! Chromer!" Teeny yells. There is a splash at the pool's tailout, then a steelhead leaps again and again. Teeny plays it to shore, examines and releases it.

Across the pool a steelhead suddenly clears water and Blood's rod bows. The fish leaps three times and is gone. Five minutes later another steelhead jumps and the fishermen in the pool— seven of them—eye the banks to see who has hooked up. Blood's rod pumps again. The fishermen go back to their fishing, watching strike indicators intently in the drift. Blood lands an eight-pound steelhead. Teeny hooks up again and lands another. The fishermen in the pool hook up and yell, or don't yell, and play steelhead after steelhead, laughing at long-line releases, or pulling free of foul-hooked fish. The hours pass, sliding easily into each other with steelhead in the air or on the bank, a surfeit of steelhead, a dreamy continuum of silver fish, easy fish, a gross national product of fish, until the gray skies turn grayer and hunger gnaws and cold hands can no longer grip leader knots.

A spin fisherman stands next to me at the head of the pool. He feeds salmon eggs down his leg and into the flow. He explains that he is fishing a small sack of eggs tied into panty hose and then dipped in borax and frozen in his freezer. His egg chum has brought the steelhead in the pool to his feet. He hooks a fish, hauls it in, bashes its head with a rock, hides the fish in the brush, and returns to catch another—this is spin fishing on Cattaraugus Creek.

LEFTY KREH: NOBILITY ONSTREAM

Lefty Kreh lost his father in 1932, when he was six. In the 1950s fishing writer Joe Brooks became his father figure. Brooks, in two decades as fishing editor for *Outdoor Life*, became the father figure of American fly fishing: The spiritual son has since become the new father figure.

In the summer of 1981 I fished the Buffalo Ford in Yellowstone Park with Lefty and my son. As usual, Lefty spent the afternoon teaching. As I sat watching from a bluff above Le Hardy Rapids, he patiently taught the techniques of shallow nymphing to schools of cutthroat trout finning obliviously at his student's feet. It was difficult to tell who was having more fun, the teacher or the student. Later, as we drove through Hayden Valley and its herds of roadside buffalo and people, Lefty spotted two bull moose feeding in a shallow lake.

"Stop the car!" he shouted. I pulled onto a shoulder and we grabbed cameras and began shooting. He taught photography to us for a while before spotting two nearby women hopelessly fiddling with point-and-shoot cameras. The rest is predictable to anyone who knows Mr. Kreh: Half an hour later he was still teaching those women how to use their cameras, while we pleaded for a departure.

That evening Lefty took a youngster aside at the Federation of Fly Fishers Conclave in West Yellowstone and taught him casting until dark. He has been doing that at conclaves for some thirty years.

I learned my casting from Lefty Kreh, Mel Krieger, and Lee and Joan Wulff. And I learned my values from all of them. But I have learned the most about *giving* from this man, for he has taught the gift of fly fishing to the world as an expression of selfless joy.

His message is: First learn; then teach. Don't express knowledge . . . share it. The knowledge that he shares is the product of his seventy-six years, most of which he has spent as a professional fly-fishing (and traditional fishing) writer. It is important to know that he survived as a child of the Depression, in a fatherless family on welfare. And it is important to know that he survived World War II and the bloodiest battle of the western front, the Battle of the Bulge, as a forward artillery observer. His values were forged in fire.

I said to Lefty once that I felt each day was an opportunity to enjoy life. "That's exactly how I feel," he responded. The difference is that he proves it, openly, overtly, and with an energy that astonishes and overwhelms the world through which he passes.

Lefty has become known as the master of the smooth, tight-looped, long-line cast. His talents in the micro-second wrist and slinging line and his performer's presence on stage mesmerize audiences. But spend time with him onstream and in his home and other extraordinary, important talents shine forth.

He is a sucker for children. No adult can compete for his attention when they are around—he *must teach them*. Onstream he is the master of *the fishing cast*. The best-kept secret in fly fishing is casts that are intentionally destroyed to catch fish, particularly trout. How to destroy straight-line casts to eliminate drag is the obscure accomplishment of the professional fly fishers. Like golfers, they "drive for show and putt for dough."

British fly-fishing writer John Goddard, whom Lefty calls the best trout fisherman he has ever seen, told me an anecdote about Lefty on the River Kennett. Goddard said there was a large brown trout there that no one could catch. It lay in a particularly difficult spot to which it was virtually impossible to present the fly without drag.

Goddard showed him the fish and Lefty cast to it. "Bloody hell," Goddard said, "he caught that trout on his first cast. No one else could have made that presentation, only Lefty."

Of course Kreh can have the first shot on any water to which he is invited. That is not what occurs. He obeys the rules: His students fish the waters first. I have seen him repeatedly give the first shots to others on tarpon, striped bass, king salmon, and other gamefish. He practices hallowed rules: Let your guest or your student go first; share the water; share your flies; share your knowledge; laugh at adversity onstream and off. Leap early to greet the day, for it may be your last opportunity to share the joy.

There have been noble men and women in the sport of fly fishing—Haig-Brown, Joe Brooks, and the Wulffs are among them. But if nobility has a face, it is Lefty Kreh. He gives the ancient values of fly fishing new, living meaning. In an age when the rules of the road—and the stream—have become frayed, we should emulate his example of life.

CARL RICHARDS: THE PURSUIT OF PERFECTION

We motored quietly in the humid darkness along a river near Tampa Bay, Florida. Dock lights illuminated the river channel to the left and right.

"Look back under the dock beneath the lights. See those black shapes chasing back and forth? Those are snook busting bait. The lights attract the bait and the bait attracts the snook. Shoot your cast back under there and strip hard."

I had tied on the latest Carl Richards saltwater baitfish imitation, a 1/0 created from a molded epoxy used by dentists. I shot the fly back under the pilings and stripped hard and fast. A black shape shot from the shadows and grabbed the fly. I had to horse the fish hard, away from the pilings and toward the boat. I had the five-pounder at the boat quickly and we moved up the river, searching each lighted dock for marauding snook.

We had fished the backcountry that day and, after naps, fished the night. Richards, a Grand Rapids, Michigan, dentist, was just retired and exploring exciting new worlds—the Ten Thousand Islands of Florida's west coast. It was not enough for Carl to explore them for their fish—snook, tarpon, jacks—he was driven to solve their food-chain preferences. He had collected all the shrimp and baitfish inhabiting that unspoiled continental shelf where A. W. Dimock (*The Book of Tarpon*) found original sport a century ago. Carl had discovered materials to imitate them realistically, in ways that no one else had attempted. Richards proudly unveiled his two years of innovation, flies that looked so real that they might fool a fellow shrimp or baitfish. They were simply the latest Richards inventions, creations that emulated nature in new ways.

Richards had begun his fly-fishing career while practicing dentistry, but he soon made it clear that fixing teeth was a means to get to trout streams. With plastics salesman Doug Swisher he had studied Michigan stream entomology under the influence of Ernest Schwiebert Jr., and the Swisher-Richards team had taken matching the hatch to new levels.

Richards, by all accounts, was a driven man. His cellar was furnished with tanks filled with rocks and flowing water. Into these special hatcheries he introduced aquatic insects—mayflies in the early years, then caddis in later decades.

Richards's day was long, eight hours in the office filling teeth, and buying and selling stocks by phone, followed by four hours in the cellar studying the life cycles of insects and photographing them in their watery world. The Swisher-Richards no-hackle flies are our legacy.

He had not lost steam. There at the edge of the nation's last great wilderness he was excited about new discoveries. He would not be denied the solving of these latest aquatic ecosystem riddles. One cannot rub shoulders with Dr. Carl Richards without being drawn into the obsessions of a perfectionist.

CHARLIE MECK: HATCHES AS WISDOM

"Look at that! It's a Green Drake! I've never seen one here this late in the season!" On the banks of Spruce Creek a man dashes to his car, pops the trunk, grabs a butterfly net, and runs back to the stream. He waves it in the air, brings the net down, reaches in, and withdraws a No. 10 mayfly with a white body.

"It *is* a Green Drake! My goodness, who would have thought it!" A childlike joy spreads across Charlie Meck's face, as though nature had at last revealed its most intimate secret to him. He is sixty-seven years old and still searching. No one has written more about the aquatic insects, the hatches of fly fishing. No one has pursued them on the North American rivers with more passion. No one has slept so restlessly, brooding that something might be hatching undetected and unrecorded *somewhere*.

One evening while I fished with Ross Purnell on an intimate little stream near my home, a nice mayfly humidity settled on the water under hemlocks lining the water. A trout rose diffidently here and there but they otherwise lay quiet, off the fin and waiting for something.

The first mayfly fluttered off the water as an evening shade crept into the woods. Another identical Size 12 mayfly settled to the water, shuddered spasmodically, and was taken quickly by a trout. Slowly then the mayflies filled the air, some descending to the water to drop egg packets, others popping to the surface to take wing. My companions and I watched the stream come to life with trout, which rose with abandon to the large, plump morsels above them. Up and down the stream, in the small eddies and runs, trout rises dimpled the stream surface.

"Is that a Green Drake hatch?" Ross inquired.

"I don't think so; the body of the spinner is not white," I said. "It's the right size, though. Maybe it's a Green Drake of another color phase. I don't know."

We caught trout, lots of trout, as the hatch continued and the fish fed eagerly in their good fortune. A Size 12 Adams did the trick, and the trout rose to it in preference to the naturals drifting nearby. I had never caught trout at will, but I did that night. I had never caught all the trout I saw rise. But I did that night. And when we reluctantly departed, trudging up through ancient hemlocks to the car, I knew that a stream would seldom offer more. But was it a Green Drake hatch that had treated us so well?

I called Charlie Meck the next day and explained the strange hatch, about the same size as the Green Drake but olive-gray in color.

"Oh, that's probably the *Siphloplecton basale*," Charlie said. And of course he was right. Meck has been relentless exploring the hatches of Pennsylvania; only he could have instantly identified the *Siphloplecton* as the relatively rare mayfly I fished to that evening.

Meck is enthralled with the adult stage of the mayflies. He carries a butterfly net but he does not carry a kick-net. He spends as much time onstream examining aquatic insects as he does fishing. He has become the Johnny Appleseed of hatch match-ers, describing to the world the aquatic insects of each trout stream from the Northeast to the Northwest. He is a friend, and a mentor.

These are but a few of my many fly-fishing mentors. To become a mentor a man must impart knowledge, understanding, and, most importantly, wisdom. He must *teach*—not just the mechanical skills of fly fishing, but the music that fills the space between the notes. When I began my fly fishing I heard the libretto, the words. The mentors taught me to hear the music.

Chapter Nine

A. Hassall. 01.

The Tenth Level

Now when I return in October to Workman's Brook on my farm in the Berkshires, I walk its banks and search for the small bare spots where the brookies have fanned in spawning play. There are so few spots that I must search for one, for the years of acid snow and rain have taken their toll and the brookies are a memory in both spirit and reality. On those searches I wonder how far I have come and how much will be left to my grandchildren. I also wonder then what it means to travel a path that few follow, one that has far different rewards than those earned by traditional fishers. What is it that separates fly fishers from other worlds? What, in the end of their travels, allows them to reach the physical and spiritual plateau I think of as the Tenth Level?

Fly fishers come to their sport for many reasons. For Ernest G. Schwiebert Jr. it is the pursuit of aesthetics—beauty. For Mel Krieger it is perfection in the cast and the Zen-like peace and escape found in those places where trout thrive. For Lefty Kreh it is the unbroken happiness in the pursuit of fish on a fly, the perfections one achieves in those journeys, and the passing of knowledge to others. In the end, the Tenth Level is a state of mind, emotional tranquillity in the knowledge and skills of the art and the ability to enter the stream spiritually. At this level the fly fisher's shadow has merged with the stream. I cannot mention all those who have reached the nirvana of our sport, but I have described a few whom I have come to know. And here are a few others who embody those admirable qualities.

Some fly fishers have advantages in reaching the Tenth Level. Their physical abilities set them apart. Their hunting instincts drive them. Their grace under fire sets them apart from the rest of us.

Steve Rajeff tied in a red saddle hackle, completed the fly with a grizzly hackle, and hand-whipped the finish. An hour later

The Tenth Level

—

Kendall the guide had us up on step and we skimmed down the east side of Exuma toward Sandy Point.

The sun burned under a cobalt sky across a glassy sea as we neared a rocky point, and the guide cut the engine and we glided into the lee of the island. We stood watching there as the sun climbed and illuminated a lagoon where a large, dark mass of fish lay suspended over a white coral-sand bottom. The breathless morning air hung like a damp warm shirt over the lagoon's aquamarine water. I saw a long slim shape lying suspended near the school of fish.

"Bonefish, barracuda," Kendall whispered. "You want them?"

"Okay. It's a little early in the tide for the permit," Rajeff replied.

The guide poled the skiff into a crescent-shaped cove and we eased over the side into tepid water. We waded across firm sand toward the dark mass of fish. An iguana scurried across the island rocks and disappeared without looking back. Rajeff shot a long clean cast seventy feet toward the pack of bonefish. The No. 4 Gotcha made a small splash where it landed. He waited for the fly to sink, then suddenly lifted his rod tip. The bonefish ran crazily away from the pack. The thin shape shot forward and intercepted it in a thrashing of water mixed with blood.

The dark mass of bonefish moved slowly away from the lagoon and the blood toward a long white flat that lay shimmering in the midday sun. Kendall poled slowly along its edge. The tide pushed gently across a clean coral sandbank. Way out, where the surface shimmered with the tide's movement, something dark moved. "Permit," Kendall whispered.

He poled hard. Rajeff stood silently on the bow, knees bent in a high, stiff crouch.

The five permit moved, feeding away from us along the sandbank, waiting for the tide to sweep food to them off its edge.

Kendall poled harder, closing the distance. His breath came in quick, urgent gasps. At about 120 feet he slowed, poling silently, easing toward the feeding fish angling upcurrent into the soft flow of the tide, moving from right to left.

Rajeff flicked the rod low and hard and shot line on the first backcast. He hauled half the line to the rear on the second then drove the 10-weight hard forward, and it arced down into the butt. The line shot in a clean, tight loop, knifing through the air toward the permit. The end shot up through the guides and out the tip-top.

The Merkin plopped just to the right of the feeding fish and drifted naturally across white sand toward the dark moving shapes. The inside fish charged and inhaled it. Rajeff pulled the line hard with his left hand and reared back on the rod with his right. The permit bolted away down the flat and the line sliced into the glare and made a clean ripping sound. The reel played out line smoothly and silently. Fifteen minutes later he held a twenty-pound fish for photos.

"You'll never see a better cast than that on any fish," I said to Kendall.

It was not the only time I had witnessed that level of fishing from Rajeff. The twelve-time world champion had earned a reputation as the best competition caster of all time, but there had been whispered suggestions that his fishing skills did not match his casting. He guided me one day on the Brooks River in Alaska and I watched as he picked off one rainbow after another, sight fishing to them as they lay feeding on sockeye eggs in thin, clear water. He targeted fish and hooked them easily with one cast after another. He was not performing then; he was enjoying himself the way a seasoned guide conducts ablutions in his off hours, on stream and alone.

Rajeff is a supremely private person, a self-assured athlete who has reached the top of his game. He does not discuss his fishing. He has no need; he is secure internally and externally.

Al Caucci shuffles his foot upcurrent of a kick-net at the Junction Pool on the East Branch of the Delaware. He lifts the net and scrapes it into a white petrie dish. Then he selects a wiggling nymph and places it on a white card.

"See, three tails; it's a mayfly nymph. But which one? It's about twelve millimeters long; see the head, it has pincerlike tusks—it's a burrower. See the double hacklelike gills protruding from the abdomen? It's a *Potomanthus* nymph. Now let's find a match for it in the fly box."

He picks out a gray nymph twelve millimeters long and places it beside the natural on the card. It is nearly an exact match.

"That's how to match the hatch here. Now let's walk over there to the other branch and see what its bottom has to offer."

Caucci walks fifty feet, kicks the bottom again, and refills the petrie dish, this time with many creepy crawlies from the stream bottom.

"See how much more there is here? The West Branch has a richer aquatic insect biota than the East Branch. That's one reason why the dry-fly fishing is so good. More species of insects—more hatches."

Caucci has been conducting his stream-bottom surveys for over three decades, from Vermont to Montana. He (and his partner Bob Nastasi) reads streams the way others read books. He understands what he reads, and when he reports his findings to local trout clubs, he often hurts feelings, for some streams are not as fertile insect habitats as their guardians believe.

Caucci understands that each trout stream has its own insect footprint. He and co-author Bob Nastasi (*Hatches* and *Hatches II*) have spent their adult lives tracking stream footprints. They have taken matching the hatch to its ultimate level—advanced amateur aquatic entomology. Others have become so enthralled with this discipline that fishing becomes a secondary, and less important, pursuit. Not so with Caucci and Nastasi. Their Comparadun patterns, with the Swisher-Richards and the Marinaro designs, revolutionized dry-fly fishing.

On stream Caucci picks his fly and casts accurately to a foam line. He picks off trout whose riseforms are unseen by the untrained eye. He concentrates on large fish, preferring to leave the others to feed unmolested. His movements are measured, unhurried, and without wasted motion. When fishing, he has the assured motion of the professional athlete.

Caucci spends a month fishing the rivers of Montana. He spends another fishing the flats of Andros Island for bonefish. He spends all year fighting for assured minimum trout survival flows for the Delaware River. He is the paradigm fly-fishing conservationist, David fighting the New York City water-management

Goliath with the slingshot of public opinion. He tweaks our conscience.

Gary Borger calls. "John, are you interested in something very controversial for the magazine?"

"Yes. What is it?"

"Have you ever heard of the *sound footprint* used by fish to locate prey?"

"Only the soundwave location explained to me by George Harvey and demonstrated by Joe Humphries in 1981. Is that what you mean, Gary?"

Harvey discovered that he could tie a fly with a large flared wing to create a shock wave in the water. At night when the fly is retrieved trout locate it by sensing the water shock wave through their lateral line. They follow the shock wave and inhale the fly as prey. Humphries demonstrated the technique for me one night in the stream at the end of his lawn. It worked on large brown trout. It was on the Harvey design of fly that Joe one night caught his Pennsylvania-record brown trout.

"Yes, but what I discovered fishing the Amazon for piarra is more dramatic. My son Jason and I could not get the piarra to take our flies because they would not make enough sound in the water when they were retrieved. We had to redesign our flies entirely to create a larger sound footprint. When we got the fly design right, the piarra were all over it, as many as one hundred hookups per day. As you can imagine, this new approach to fly design will raise some blood pressures."

Borger has been "raising some blood pressures" for a long time. Back in the late 1970s he visited the Letort Spring Run in Carlisle, Pennsylvania, and caught some very large wild browns using, ahem, a strike indicator and a strip-leech fly. No one knows what Vince Marinaro thought of this bravado, or whether he ever knew of it. Suffice it to say, in fly fishing's pantheon of values an enshrined golden rule was trampled, in the very spot where a dry-fly high priest had proclaimed it.

Borger, perhaps fly fishing's most articulate and well-informed practitioner, proceeded to catch large trout on the hallowed waters, Armstrong's Spring Creek, and the Railroad Ranch on the Henry's Fork of the Snake River, all on his rabbit-strip leech.

What are we to say about this behavior? Fly fishers worldwide have become famous for their sporting self-restraint. English sporting etiquette demands that gentlemen fish only on the surface with dry flies fished upstream and only to rising trout. Have these essentially nineteenth-century rules of the British gentry endured under the strain of modern usage, when the rules of the road have been subjected to all manner of road rage?

Borger is the most conscientious of fly fishers, an innovative fly tier, a casting instructor, a catch-and-release fisher who uses only barbless hooks. But some old rules have changed of late. Some fly fishers employ egg imitations, unheard of, or condoned, four decades ago. Strike indicators, another modern innovation, have made nymphing possible for the hordes of those newly arrived on the streams of the world, and on hallowed steelhead rivers they have made success rates so high that proposals to ban them have caused hot debates. On the waters of New Zealand flies tied with anything but natural materials are banned by law. On the trout streams of Germany catching and *releasing* trout is illegal. Lee Wulff believed that fishing for Atlantic salmon beneath the top four inches of water should be banned, and the lower water be proclaimed a refuge for the fish. Some anglers believe that a Clouser Deep Minnow is not a fly, just a jig. Others demand that the Woolly Bugger be banned from all waters.

How, then, can one be ethical in a world scorched by political correctness? Borger is at ease with his behavior. He is a hunter of fish and he hunts them with ethical tools—flies that can be cast on a fly rod and that imitate foods fish eat. He releases his fish healthy and unharmed. He carries no cultural guilt that endows the fish with humanlike emotions. He does not entertain the anthropomorphic thought that *if fish could scream in terror, would we fish?* because they cannot, and the thought that they might is an ontological absurdity. In Borger's world some fish seek their prey using a sound footprint; therefore the hunter of fish on a fly designs a pattern that will create that footprint. He will then catch that fish. The catch will be a consummation of his hunt.

Bob Popovics coats a Surf Candy with five-minute epoxy. He slowly rotates the head of his vise so the epoxy, which sags to the bottom of the hook, resumes its position of equilibrium. He adds more with his bodkin and inserts it between the fibers of yellow and white Super Hair. He continues the rotation until the fly's head is firm and as clean and clear as glass. Then he adds prism eyes, positioning them carefully on the epoxy behind the hook eye. With the addition of the eyes, the fly seems, magically, to take life.

Popovics is ready. He will head for the shore outside Barnegat Bay where the stripers are crashing bait at the inlet jetty or the bluefish are on a blitz herding bunker into the shallows in a savage debauch. His Surf Candy, exact in every detail and radiating light through its translucency, will be eaten for the real thing, menhaden, sand eels, or some other bait that frequents the places where the ocean meets the land.

Popovics is the father of saltwater matching-the-bait. He is to the shoreline what Ronalds, Schwiebert, Richards and Swisher, and Caucci and Nastasi are to the trout streams. His flies, created from modern synthetics, epoxies, and glue, are nearly identical in size, color, and shape to the baits on which stripers, bluefish, and other saltwater gamefish prey.

Popovics has paid his dues: He has labored in the vineyards of fishing and fly tying for thirty years, perfecting skills that attract hundreds to his weekly fly-tying classes. The six-foot-three former Marine haunts the shorelines from Massachusetts to New Jersey, firing eighty-foot casts to the surf, in the night when the stripers prowl the shallows at Menemsha or Montauk. He is at

Point Lookout when the false albacore arrive. His wrists and hands have swollen from carpal tunnel syndrome, the result of pounding pizza at his restaurant or of casting to the sea. He casts and retrieves repeatedly, hand over hand, into a stripping basket at his waist. When the blitzes are on, or the stripers have arrived at Chatham, he will take and release from ten to fifty fish in twelve hours of fishing. He and his bleary-eyed companions stagger home to sleep fitfully for brief hours, then tie flies urgently before again stumbling shoreward to catch the tide.

When the bonito enter Menemsha Harbor at first light, they come fast. You can see them round the jetty as the outgoing tide draws water and sand eels from the salt pond. The bonito race crazily back and forth across the harbor, their takes exploding like small grenades in the moving slick. The eighty-foot casts to them must be made from the jetties. Few men can make those casts with 10-weights and shooting heads and superslick running lines cast from shooting baskets handmade from plastic tubs drilled and epoxied with hundred-pound monofilament quills to prevent the line from blowing in the wind. This is high cult stuff, and the fly-fishing surf jocks are here annually to meet the fish on their equinoctial movement southward. One senses that his immersion in this orbicular movement of hemispheres and fish, is the closest that he will ever come to a participation in cosmology.

The committed instinctively stay close to Popovics. He has mastered what is important—the size, shape, color, and action of the flies; the right matching of lines, knots, monofilaments; the lore of tidal rips and jetties, when the largest stripers will hold in those places where waves crash and men who dare them may suddenly be swept away. These risks, these prices, some fly fishers will endure to discover and rediscover a place of natural happiness near the sea where fish hunt their food. The margin of the ocean belongs to the fish, and to them.

The eucalyptus trees that surround the Golden Gate Casting Club in San Francisco help to break the winds that sweep in from the Pacific. They also give an air of Olympian majesty to the place that has produced fly fishing's greatest competitive casters. It is also the place where I began to understand the complex inner mysteries of the cast.

To make his points Mel Krieger must demonstrate, either with his hands or with a fly rod. He inscribes an arc in the air with the rod.

"You must stop the rod to form the loop. The casting arc de-temines the length of your stroke. In other words, for a short cast you make a short stroke and a short arc and for a long cast you make a long arc. Watch my casting hand and the rod."

He makes a short, quick stroke.

"See, I'm casting off the tip of the rod, a short, quick stroke and a small casting arc. Now let me show you the long cast."

He pops out line on the casting pool, hauls a backcast with a long pull of his line hand, reaches back with the rod into a long, open arc, then comes forward, stops the rod hard, and launches the entire line down the pool.

"Okay!" he exclaims with a released inner joy. He stops to savor the feeling that the cast has released within him. He smiles and throws a kiss to the wind.

"That's a long arc and a long cast. Let's see you make one. Remember, you must open the arc, and when you stroke, you must stop the rod hard—*whump* it. When you make this cast you should feel the rod load down into the butt."

I attempt to load the rod too strongly and my timing is bad and the cast tails badly. But there is hope for my casting and Krieger works with me throughout the afternoon. Gradually I begin to feel the timing, to learn that casting is not strength. Inherently I begin to change, psychologically first then physically.

I must change my physical mind memory, but before I can change it, I must image the cast. I must *see* what my body must do before I can do it.

Watching Krieger and the Rajeffs (Steve has a brother, Tim, who is also a world-class caster) cast helps me image the cast. I watch them intensely, perfect physical machines driving lines down the quiet lagoons of the Golden Gate Casting Club. It will be years before I can do it correctly, years of practice. Strangely, it will be years of inner evaluation before the *spirit* of the cast becomes apparent to me and I can feel the inner life of a graphite rod and the magic that is there to be released by my hand.

In the end, when I have learned the lessons taught to me by Mel Krieger, Lefty Kreh, and Joan Wulff, I realize that the soul of fly fishing lies within the fly cast, and within the rod that the fly fisher energizes to make it. Now when I fish my pleasure is as much in the casting as it is in the catching of fish. It is as if the catching is a conclusion of all the physical and emotional preparation that has preceded it.

Ernest G. Schwiebert's *Matching the Hatch* (1955) was greeted by most angling writers as revelation, the vade mecum of American fly-fishing entomology. To read its foreword is to discover the spirit that lives in the heart of all fly fishers. Schwiebert wrote: "Trout fishing is an art; and like the other arts, it is greatly enhanced by the history and romance that have accumulated over the centuries. The rivers that were the stage for much of this angling drama have something that is lacking on other less fabled rivers."

In this foreword Schwiebert traces the important developmental literature of the sport of fly fishing. And he makes it clear that he has attempted to discover the resting places of those men whose printed instructions fed his passion for the sport. No one has more reverence for fly fishing than Schwiebert.

So who is this man, this scholar of fly fishing, its origins, and its twentieth-century development? And what has his role been in that evolution?

It is important to know that Ernest G. Schwiebert is a scholar with a doctorate in architectural history from Princeton University. It is also important to know that he is the son of the late Ernest G. Schwiebert, Ph.D., a fly fisher and professional historian with a specialty in Martin Luther and the Reformation. Schwiebert senior wrote his last book on the Reformation at the age of eighty-five, and saw it published at the age of one hundred.

The elder Schwiebert introduced his son to fly fishing before he was ten. Little did the father realize what he had unleashed on the streams, for the young Schwiebert began turning over rocks and discovering entomological secrets before he was twelve. With the help of Bill Blades he quickly became a master fly tier, and with the help of Wittenberg College professor Dr. E. T. Bodenberg, and a legendary photographic memory, he began his journey as an amateur stream entomologist. The making of a modern archetypal fly fisher had begun.

Schwiebert's lifelong love of fly fishing and its practitioners fills his books, from *Matching the Hatch*, to *Nymphs*, the two-volume *Trout*, and his essays in *Remembrances of Rivers Past*. He is currently working on revised editions of *Nymphs* and *Matching the Hatch*, and he has completed unpublished manuscripts on the North Branch of the Umpqua and Alaska. He also writes frequently on architectural history. Schwiebert is the most extensively published author in the history of fly fishing.

It is fly fishing that makes him tick. When I first saw him at a Winchester Arms shoot for outdoor writers in 1957, Lee Wulff referred to him as "the heir apparent." Wulff considered the twenty-six-year-old to be the crown prince of fly-fishing writing. In many ways Schwiebert fulfilled that promise.

In his writings Schwiebert portrays the values, the glue, that hold a spiritual brotherhood together. He expounds on those values because he believes in them passionately. If he is anything, he is an idealist who wears his heart on his sleeve in print, and who believes that "Ours is the grandest sport. It is an intriguing battle of wits between the angler and the trout; and in addition to appreciating the tradition and grace of the game, we play it in the magnificent out-of-doors."

I worked with Schwiebert and his manuscripts from 1978 to 1981. One cannot work closely with a man and his writing without acquiring an understanding of his ideals. It became apparent to me, in editing his work, that Schwiebert adores fly fishing as an end rather than a means. He worships those men and women who have taken its pursuits to the level of art. He idealizes those who have achieved the Tenth Level, that combination of supreme skill, grace, and intellectual understanding that achieves spiritual beauty.

Schwiebert popularized matching the hatch. In effect, he gave it life by describing, in greater detail than had been attempted previously, the intricate web of insect life that exists on and beneath the water and how trout feed on it for survival. Schwiebert must share honors with his predecessors Preston Jennings (*A Book of Trout Flies*, 1935) and particularly Vincent C. Marinaro (*A Modern Dry Fly Code*, 1950), and with his followers—Swisher-Richards, Caucci-Nastasi, LaFontaine, and Meck.

What all of this is leading to is what Marinaro found so in-triguing. He quotes Colonel E. W. Harding from the *The Fly Fisher and the Trout's Point of View* in chapter 1 of his *Modern Dry Fly Code* as follows:

> To some this may seem like taking a recreation far too seriously. If these objectors can take lightly the sense of baf-fled disappointment following on failure by the waterside; if they are content to enjoy success as though it were some caprice of chance; if, in short, they are content to be slaves and not the masters of their fishing fate, then perhaps they are right: but to me the sense of bafflement robs me of half my pleasure and casual unexplained success is but Dead Sea fruit to the palate of enjoyment.

Marinaro says: "That statment deserves the stamp of immor-tality. It contains the fundamental philosophy of the fly fisher-man and it expresses the best justification, if any is needed, for further complicating the fascinating art of fly fishing."

Marinaro is right, of course. And these statements reveal the Golden Thread to which the poet John Donne alludes in his poem and that I use in the prologue of this book. (He meant the pursuit of God.) Not satisfied to accept success as caprice, the Tenth Level fly fishers I describe have sought the answers. Unexplained success is Dead Sea fruit. They want explanations and they pursue them, throughout their lives, on salt water and on fresh. They are the searchers for truth, the innovators, the hunters, the empiricists. For them the search *is* the sport.

There is one other characteristic of these fly fishers worth mention: They are *happy*. They find a contentment that comes from engagement, from the pursuit of perfection in forms and understanding. They remind me of music lovers, professionals who are compelled to pursue a sound or the perfection to be found in the inborn beauty of an instrument played at its highest level of performance.

Is this, then, the secret of fly fishing's inner joy—the pursuit of perfection? It was for Marinaro, and it is for Schwiebert, and it is for the fly fishers I have known who have reached the Tenth Level—they are our mentors.

Chapter Ten

Literature

Does Izaak Walton deserve his place of honor as the father in fly fishing's pantheon of family figures? British author Jeremy Paxman has serious doubts.

Paxman's superb *Walton and Cotton* (1996, the Flyfisher's Classic Library boxed edition) deserves special attention, for after four hundred years of often thoughtless adoration from breathless book buyers, something more substantive is required for an adult understanding of the man (Walton) and his book

The Compleat Angler. As Paxton points out, after four hundred editions no book in the English-speaking world has been more consistently reprinted except the Bible and *Pilgrim's Progress*.

Paxman reports a number of historical truths and Walton misdemeanors that are unknown to many readers. *The Compleat Angler* was not the first book of its kind. That honor goes to the *Treatyse of Fysshynge Wyth An Angle*, part of the *Boke of St. Albans* (1496), attributed to Dame Juliana Berners. The juicy, and devastating, tidbit, discovered in 1954 by American book collector Otto von Kienbusch (the Princeton University collection) is proof that Walton plagiarized massively and completely from a 1577 book called *The Arte of Angling*. Here's what Paxman says:

> It was a sensational discovery, made particularly exciting by the curious similarities between *The Arte of Angling* and *The Compleat Angler*. These are so frequent that the case is unanswerable that Walton simply filched much of his material. He even repeats factual errors from the earlier version. More devastatingly, *The Arte of Angling*, published seventy-six years before Walton's "gem of a book," is also written in the form of a dialogue between Piscator and Viator.

Paxman goes on to point out that Walton was a bait fisherman and that Charles Cotton, the true fly fisher, added the fly-fishing content in the fifth edition of *The Compleat Angler*. None of this is news, but the historical picture and context that the author draws of the man, his time, and his work is myth-shattering.

The Paxman tome will not change the tides of literary history, although it should. *The Compleat Angler* will remain the angling book by which all others are judged, and it will remain unread by most book buyers simply because, as Ed Zern once pointed out in his superb book *To Hell with Fishing,* "If you think this book is dull, go curl up with *The Compleat Angler.* Then try to uncurl."

Which brings me to the question, "What constitutes fly-fishing *literature* in the sense of fine art?"

In the pantheon of English literature most fly-fishing instructional books are not significant; in the pantheon of fly-fishing history they are. Our well-known fly-fishing books are most often the expositional writings of exceptional fishermen who present in print, sometimes eloquently, what they have learned about our sport. Literate fly fishers cherish them, and many collect them.

But there are other fly-fishing books, ones that have higher aspirations. These books, many of them written within the past three decades, and most importantly in the past two, deserve special attention, for they achieve a level of writing that *is* fine art, and in some cases very fine.

How does one find them? I can give you my short list, but fine-art judgments are in the mind of the reader and in the end it's one man's meat. Here is a taste of what I like.

ESSAYS

Spring Creek by Nick Lyons. The best of fly-fishing literature can be found in this field of writing and this book is one of the best—and I think Nick's best. He has written many others, all exceptional writing and all must-reading if you have followed his writing career. What all the fly-fishing essayists have in common is their love of fishing and their need to discover personal verities through their sport. If Lyons has a muse, it speaks to him through his fishing and his life as a New York book publisher, writer, and retired English professor who, wistfully, wishes to escape the asphalt jungle but who is doomed to obey the beast of duty. Read all his books for the gestalt, but finish with this one.

The Habit of Rivers by Ted Leeson. Rivers are the other things
that these fine-art writers have in common. I'll let Leeson tell why:

> To some temperaments, fishing appeals most deeply as
> an approach to a web of relations that give shape and co-
> herence to the natural world. Fly fishing in particular em-
> braces the kind of minutiae that weaves themselves into
> ever enlarging contexts. A trout stream points backward to
> geology and atmospherics, to history and evolution; it leads
> forward to insects and fish, to hydrology and botany, to lit-
> erature and philosophy. Connections branch and rebranch
> in overlapping associations until finally, from a pattern of
> venation in a mayfly wing, you can reconstruct an entire
> watershed. In this regard fly fishing is entirely self-regulatory,
> for by nature it revolves around on its own most revealing
> image—the riseform. The rise of a trout to a drifting insect
> reverberates in expanding eccentric ripples, magnified itera-
> tions of a simple event that resonate outward to encompass
> more and more, remaining visible long after and far from
> the thing that made them. The rings of a rising trout even-
> tually comprehend the entire river, yet no matter how large
> their compass, like all circles they never cease to invite an
> inference of the center.

The book, a series of essays on the natural world of the fly fisher, is built around this assumption. It's the first time in fly-fishing literature that such a conceptual conceit is made—and accomplished. All things are brought, magically, and with superb writing, back to the center. The question of why we fly fish is answered.

As with all the modern writings mentioned here, the writer attempts to find deeply personal meaning in a fragmented world and finds his view of truth. The writer must have the abilities of an exceptional stylist. And he must be honest. This book fulfills our aesthetic longings.

Trout Reflections: A Natural History of the Trout and Its World by David M. Carroll is the kind of accomplishment that few of the great artists in either writing or painting have ever achieved—a double. Usually the writing slips beneath the film, or the artwork causes our teeth to ache, or both. Carroll achieves a level of both that is breathtaking. Think of what Thoreau could have created had he possessed this level of artistic talent to accompany his stunning gift with words. As a youth who grew up in the same world (western Massachusetts) that the author shared, and as a fly fisher, I find *Reflections* to be the ultimate personal artistic statement, one man's completely portrayed perception of his natural world. In the history of fly-fishing literature no one has ever reached these levels simultaneously in two fine-art fields.

San Juan River Chronicle and *Notes from the San Juan* by Steven J. Meyers needed to be written. Meyers was compelled to express what was bothering him, and more importantly he needed to find a father and a home. An easterner, he went in search of both on the trout streams of the San Juan Mountains and in the high country near Durango, Colorado. What Meyers found on the San Juan was what writer Craig Woods once described as "the river as a looking glass." Meyers's essays are reflections of the self he discovered while fishing. His stylistic ability in creating a sensual feel of time and place is so strong that I am carried compellingly along in his experiences. This is one promise and fulfillment of superb writing.

Trout Madness. In 1960 Michigan Supreme Court Justice and novelist (*Anatomy of a Murder*) John Voelker (aka Robert Traver) described himself as a fallen angel, a man who, despite the best of educations and professional training, was, alas, a trout bum. What followed was another stylistic masterpiece, a confession of one man's obsession with fly fishing—in this case in Michigan's Upper Peninsula. Traver's books deal with his experiences on and around the water with whimsical humor from the Michigan North Woods. All the Traver books rank as literature, for the author's great personal character and flair emerge in his superbly stylistic writing.

In the Ring of the Rise by Vincent C. Marinaro is a fly-fishing naturalist's view of the stream (the Letort) and the behavioral traits of the trout that inhabit it. The book was evolutionary in concept, advancing what the British author Ronalds had disclosed in his 1836 classic *The Fly Fisher's Entomology* and Goddard-Clark, in 1980, would expand in their superb *The Trout and the Fly.*

Ring is an expositional book, one that technically does not qualify as English literature, but the chapter "A Game of Nods" certainly ranks as one of the finest natural history essays ever written. A backyard encounter between a man and a trout, it portrays the obsession he has with a fish and his attempts to answer the unanswerable questions of angling. Marinaro's *A Modern Dry-Fly Code* also stands among the best, as much for the author's lawyerlike clarity of expression as for his intuitive logic. Marinaro may have been wrong in his logic of fly design, but who cares? His books stand as literature.

Trout Bum by John Gierach reminds me of *Tom Sawyer* and *Huckleberry Finn*. That's good company. Gierach has followed this book with a seemingly endless periodical parade of similar books of essays that portray the picaresque life of a modern literate trout bum. Is Gierach the 1980s–90s Voelker? You bet. And with the same kind of persona and flair. The Rocky Mountain regional flavor is strong, and the sidekick *Travels with Charlie* plots (in this case A. K.) work.

Ninety Two in the Shade, a novel by Thomas McGuane, heralded the arrival of a major new writing talent in the United States. McGuane has had successes with movie writing, short stories, and essays. While many of his stories have reflected his passion for fly fishing, McGuane does not write *about* fly fishing; he uses the sport as a backdrop for his art, as did novelists Ernest Hemingway and Norman Maclean, author of *A River Runs Through It*.

For fly fishers his 1999 collection of essays, *The Longest Silence*, may be his best. McGuane's writings head the list (with Hemingway's short stories) of literary works that in one way or another mention our sport.

In 1980 artist Russ Chatham edited *Silent Seasons*, a collection of short stories and essays by a number of excellent writers, including Jim Harrison, Jack Curtis, McGuane, Harmon Henkin, and Chatham. The writing is uniformly superb, although not uniform. Each story presents one author's perception of an aspect of fly fishing. None of the authors holds a job; all live in places where there are fish and game but few people.

As a collection of writings this is fly-fishing literature at its best. Chatham views the world through the lens of the fishing-possessed artist. He has spent his writing career trying to make the real world conform to his vision. It won't, but the artistic tension created by this conflict produces writing that is both passionate and clean. Chatham is also a superb fisherman.

A River Never Sleeps by Roderick Haig-Brown speaks to all of us because Haig-Brown has the comfortable conversational style of all great storytellers. Pages 216 through 218 reveal why he wrote and for whom. His father got Haig-Brown started hunting and fishing as a child in England, and after his father's death, an uncle taught him the classic English field skills. After an English education, Haig-Brown moved to the New World, eventually to Vancouver Island, British Columbia, where he worked as a logger, a commercial fisherman, and eventually a justice of the peace and book author.

Haig-Brown was a classic British man of the field and of letters, living and fishing on the last frontier. That life for him was a daily exploration of the possible, the challenging, and the surprising onstream, and his infectious love of the outdoors is reflected in his writing. His books earn their keep.

Ernest G. Schwiebert Jr. is known for his classic instructional book, *Matching the Hatch* (1955), but his creative writing earns a special place in fly-fishing literature. His *Remembrances of Rivers Past* and *A River for Christmas* are vintage Schwiebert. They reveal the special magic of place and beauty that he finds so compelling about the sport of fly fishing. Schwiebert has always been an admirer of Hemingway, and influences of the Hemingway style infuse his writing. Stylistically there is no writing in fly-fishing literature more evocative of place and mood than in these two books.

Must-reads: All of Charlie Waterman's writings; all of Jim Harrison's writings; all of McGuane's writings; all of Chatham's writings; all of Jack Curtis's writings; all of William Humphrey's writings; all of Steve Raymond's writings; all of Craig Nova's novels and essays; and in poetry John Engels's *Big Water*.

The best *literature* in the history of fly fishing has been written in the past three decades. Much of it has been written by American writers. We have lived the Golden Age.

DREAMS OF YESTERYEAR

Can it be that three thousand flies have virtually disappeared from our fly boxes? Can it be that names like Carrie Stevens, Preston Jennings, Ray Bergman, and Charles Defeo are no longer known in fly-fishing households? You bet. But they have gained a just renown thanks to the specialty do-it-yourself book publishers, notable among them Paul Schmookler and Ingrid Sils.

I mention them because they have created the most professionally done, most aesthetically pleasing and beautiful books in the history of fly fishing. Their books reprise for us the best of fly tying. Schmookler and Sils began their exhaustive work in book publishing with *Rare and Unusual Fly Tying Materials: A Natural History (Volumes I and II)* and followed with *Forgotten Flies.*

The Schmookler-Sils books were not for the faint of heart, small of purse, or diminutive of physical stature. They should be sold by the pound; *Forgotton Flies* weighs in at 11 pounds, 3.3 ounces, unquestionably the heaviest book in fly-fishing literature. So what's all the fuss?

The paper is as heavy as it comes in a book—eighty-pound stock—as white as a trout's belly, and it is acid-free and printed on the world's best flatbed press. The books were hand-bound (in China), and there are five hundred pages of Schmookler/Sils studio-quality color plates showing more than three thousand flies. The Schmookler offerings earned their reputations as the cream of fly-fishing books.

Who buys these books? Active fishermen are notoriously value-driven, so much so that you'd think few would pay this price of admission. But as Schmookler points out, there are some fifty thousand fly tiers worldwide who specialize in realistic and radical tying techniques, and many of them *don't fish*. They are a hobby group—*a subculture of fly tiers who do not need to fish*.

Schmookler has hit on something: Fly tying is a worldwide affinity group whose members are now tied together by the Internet. They talk to each other, and they buy high-quality, high-priced books. *Rare and Unusual Fly Tying Materials*, *Volume I*, went into a third printing and *Volume II* a second.

Austin "Mac" Francis's *Land of Little Rivers* is another self-published labor of love that no establishment publisher could afford to touch. It was simply too expensive to turn a writer loose for twenty-five years and send a world-class photographer up-country to the Catskills to snap shutters for a year. Costs be damned, Francis decided he would tell the story of the place he haunted as a fly fisher his entire life, and he got renowned photographer Enrico Ferorelli to spend a full year capturing the Catskill streams and their moods on film.

Land of Little Rivers describes the major (not the only) birthplace of American fly fishing the way no other book has, from the geology, the rivers, and their histories to the lives of fly-fishing icons Theodore Gordon, Art Flick, the Dettes, Edward Hewitt,

Harry and Elsie Darbee, George LaBranche, Joan and Lee Wulff, and the great regional bamboo rod makers Pinky Gillum, Hiram Leonard, and Everett Garrison.

The photographs of the legendary split-bamboo rods and heavily hackled drys and wets recall a gentler time when fly fishing was gaining a small foothold in post-frontier American culture. It was an era when country boys joined city socialites onstream in the Catskills to learn how to catch the new trout from Europe (browns) on dry flies. The fraternity compared notes and developed the flies that led to many of the modern offerings and adaptations we use today. These fly-fishing pioneers found their pleasures, and in many cases their livings and reputations, on the Catskill streams.

The Ferorelli landscapes echo the T. Morris Longstreth quote that opens this book: "The Catskills are a well-watered mountainland of Cooper's tales and the Psalms of David, deep forests and green peaks, no lava flows, no vast *sterilities* of sand or ice. The holy of holies, however, has always been a quiet place. Let *sublimity* stun. The heart warms easier to serenely sloping ranges and the sweet-scented streams of man's oldest pursuit."

Francis told this story of the Catskill Mountains sweetly and from his heart.

Graydon and Leslie Hilyard in *Carrie Stevens* portrayed yet another important chapter in the history of American fly fishing—the epic of the Rangeley Lakes region and its legendary fly tier Carrie Stevens. Anyone who has fished these lakes should find this book a haunting reminder that great wild fisheries spawn exceptional fly fishers and tiers. Such sporting challenges create cults of their own where necessity mothers invention; thus the greatest American streamers for lake fishing were created here. The Hilyards took a decade of their lives to research and recall for us the flies that haunted the fishing dreams of our fathers and grandfathers.

We owe the authors of these three books a debt of gratitude. At a risk far beyond any chance of fair monetary remuneration, they made huge investments in time and money to re-create worlds that had great personal meaning for them. They brought those worlds back for us, the fly fishers of the world.

A few critics have observed that the sport of fly fishing is unique in having its own literature. It is even more unique in having such a large one. No one has explained why this is so. Could it be that a televison anchorperson got it right when she said: "I think of fly fishers as poets who fish"? Perhaps fly fishing attracts men and women with artistic temperaments. If it so, we are fortunate, for some of the best fly fishing can indeed be found in print. And if the good places, the good fish, and the good experiences have value, then we need our literature to remind us why we fish—to define our shared values. I know of no better reason to start a personal library as a lifelong passion and commitment.

Chapter Eleven

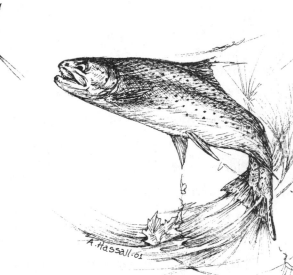

A Fly Fisher's Life List

So where will this end? Perhaps on a trout stream in the Berkshires. I feel like some nymphal insect that has gone through eight instars before discovering that it can fly. I have been on this journey for some six decades, only to discover that teaching my grandson Ben how to catch a bass has more meaning than landing a 150-pound tarpon. The experience, for children and for the man who wanders flicking a fly up a mountain stream, is a matter of context rather than the mechanics of catching fish. What has become important to me is to help him understand his place in a complex web of natural beauty. I have grown from atavistic hunter-gatherer into a voyeur bent on finding greater meaning, worthiness, immutability, and a higher value, for Ben and for myself. Now, like Plunkett-Greene, I have one river. My shadow has merged into it. Now I will take my grandson to see it.

In my dreams I take Ben fishing. I lead him up Workman's Brook to the small pools above the beaver pond. We sit on the bank then and watch the water where the brook runs through the sunlit pasture and bends to enter the pond. There we watch as a small spinner ball of *Tricorythodes* dances above the stream. A beaver swims across the pond and two whitetails, a doe and her spotted fawn, nibble quietly in the shallows where the fat weeds have gone to tassel.

There is no need to talk here; silence is a golden harvest. Sitting, my grandson may witness a luminous natural revelation, one that will be correct for his generation. For him epiphanies, begun here, can become continuous if he grasps the Golden Thread and follows the gentle path of fly fishing. If the spinners fall, for there is no guarantee that they will, trout noses may peek through the surface. We will not move to fish. Watching will be enough to make longing live in his eyes until he is old. He will experience many suggestions of natural harmony, and he will know what we all know, and search to confirm, that the insect (possibly an ancient *Tricorythodes*) drowns forever in amber, in "a piece of cough drop sucked by time." This context, this special immortality, is the fly fisher's sweetest love. It is imbibed in his youth and sucked like candy throughout his life.

This first music my grandson may not hear distinctly, but his inner ear is learning a lifelong balance from his eyes. Slowly, fly fishing will become his equilibrium. He may first come to love the dip of a bobber, then the nod of a trout, to know them as markers of his inner horizon. He may become an intruder into silences. He may discover a cosmic symmetry, an inference that fish are part of a circadian rhythm.

I took him once to a small pond to fish sunfish with a bobber. The fish hung in amber suspension ogling the worm. A slight tug on the line enticed one forward to nibble. When it bit, the bobber nodded, then dipped.

"Lift the rod, Ben!" I yelled. And the fish was on and he reeled until the little sunny flopped on the beach at his feet and he declined to touch it. I recalled then my childhood fear of live, finny fish.

"Hold her around the middle like this, Ben, so the sharp dorsal fin won't prick you. Fold the fin down along the back; keep it under your hand but don't squeeze too hard—her belly is delicate and you can injure her. See the eyes? These are the gill covers and here inside are the gills. The fish uses them to take oxygen from the water and breathe. This is the dorsal fin, and these are the pectoral fins; they are like your arms. Fish have no hands, so they must taste every floating thing with their mouths to see if it is food or not. This is a female sunfish. See how fat her belly is with eggs? She's ready to spawn. Let's let her go."

"Can't we keep her to take home, Grandpa?"

"See this sign here, Ben? It says 'Catch and Release Fishing.' We must release her. Anyway, it's best to release her so there will be more fish here for another day."

As the sun rose higher, we hooked sunfish, and largemouth bass cruised by in the clear water and, spurred by the struggling, tried to eat them. Then the bobber dove deep and ran without bobbing.

"Let it run, Ben. Don't lift yet."

The bobber ran away under water toward an overhanging bush along a nearby shore and stopped.

"Okay, lift now, Ben." The little boy lifted and the line went tight. He struggled to reel until the line sang like a bowstring. Then the bobber came in slowly as Ben fought to reel line. Trailing behind it was a mass of weeds and somewhere in that mass a largemouth bass.

"Back up now, Ben. Reel! Bring it up on shore."

Ben hauled back on the rod. He pulled the flopping bass onto the sandy shore and we grabbed for it.

"See here, Ben? See the tail sticking there deep in the bass's throat? That's your sunfish. The bass ate it after it took your worm. This is a largemouth bass."

"It's Big Charlie, Grandpa!"

"Yes, Ben. See how its lip extends to the back of its eye here? This fish is about four pounds. Remember I said that big fish eat small fish?"

I watched Ben then, fishing. I watched him closely, searching for that inner compulsion to hunt. If that fulgurite is not in him, he will not take the Golden Thread, for all fishermen are hunters in their hearts, and they must fish to reach their horizons.

Far from Workman's Brook I have my new personal river near my home. It is a little one, a bottom-flow freestoner that winds through a green wooded valley whose mountains run like hogbacks extending from east to west. Some twist of tectonic fate has made this geo-logic to confuse me, for I have lived my life where mountains run north and south. My mental compass is confused; I am disoriented until I reach the stream, which runs in perfect silence under hemlocks except for the sighing of the wind in the bows.

It is summer and the hatches have run their course, from the tiny black caddis and olives through the succulent Ephemeridae and into the chitinous terrestrials. In these woods there is no trico to set the table each morning for the trout. Only the inch-worms dangling from the hemlocks to the water and the ants, ci-cadas, and beetles feed the trout, which have been placed there by a fish commission anxious to sell licenses.

The trout are not easy; they have seen it all. The fly fishers who sneak along these paths from pool to pool are experienced Pennsylvanians, fly fishing's best. They are equipped with the finest rods that modern alchemists can produce, six- to eight-foot graphites that can throw a line a hundred feet. Their tippets are as thin as spider filament, as clear as glass, and as strong as dental floss. Things have changed since I was boy and split-cane rods threw lines too slowly yet gently.

Some writers have mourned the loss of these amiable tools—the Gillum, Leonard, Powell, Garrison, and Winston works of art. But I have learned to love the graphites as newer, more efficient forms of the same art and no less pleasing. On this little stream, where an eight-foot 4-weight graphite can sling line in a tunnel, I love the challenge of picking brush pockets on my backcasts and shooting tight loops under limbs.

They say in this valley that you can use any fly in summer as long as it's a green inchworm, for the natural is what the trout feed on, along with black ants and beetles. You must dress in camouflage and sneak along the bank trail and watch ahead for trout on the fin. It will do no good to fish to trout that lay doggo, as though sulking or asleep. (Trout *sleep*. I poked one with my rod once in three inches of clear water on the Paloma River in Chile. And I spotted a sleeping trout in lake shallows in Tasmania. There are no winged predators for the trout to fear, so they rest easy in the clear water.)

Fishing here is very private. No one can see more than fifty feet; you are alone; it's as though you are fishing in a wooded closet where the trees sigh. This hidden stream, whose destination is the river that the Susquehannocks called the Muddy, whose destination is the Chesapeake Bay, down streaming to the Atlantic, is mine.

Of course it is not *mine*—I have no deed to it. One cannot own a stream. Fly-fishing writers have appropriated the nearly sacred "beloved" to describe the attachment that the Plunkett-Greenes and Haig-Browns of our sport have felt for their chosen waters. Can one love a river? If in your relationship to a stream you have known commitment, devotion, affection, ardor, tenderness, passion, patience, and growing understanding, then it *is yours*.

Haig-Brown *loved* his Campbell River (on Vancouver Island where he lived) intimately. That intimacy grew in part from familiarity—he lived along its shores and fished it year-round. In no other way can a man take a river into his heart. He must be near it; he must have reasons to visit it in spring, when it awakens with the spawning runs (steelhead on the Campbell) and in summer when the main runs of salmon arrive, and in fall when they slowly die and the river prepares itself for the winter that will follow. He will visit it in winter, too, for he knows that the early- and late-run steelhead may be holding in the runs and holes and he can dispel his discontent with one tight line and one bright leaping fish.

His first instinct is to catch the fish. He pursues them with imperfect skills, but he soon learns where the fish prefer to hide. He then discovers, slowly, how to cast, how to present the flies that steelhead and salmon love most, and how to play large, powerful fish when they are hooked and run deep into his backing and leap to throw the hook.

This is all very fine, enough for most men who chase the fish of the world from honey hole to honey hole like lotus eaters dipping nectar. But for the true lover of rivers, and especially the man of one river, the moving water is his teacher and his lover. If his haunt is a trout stream with a smorgasbord of hatches, he learns them, for they set the trout's table throughout the season. The emerging insects become his book of angling days. He learns that when the shadbush blooms the Hendricksons appear, and when the corn tassels and the daylilies have gone to seed, the tricos will appear each morning above the stream, and each evening *Ephoron leukon*, the White Fly, will fill the air above the darkening river and bring the fish up to sip. He knows that the grasshoppers will soon come to the river and then the flying ants will arrive. He will by then have grown to know that his river is a living thing. He has learned the derivation and the meaning of *Ephemera*. He has also learned that ephemeral beings are delicate and that they disappear when streams are charged with man-made chemicals.

This man's stream has become his teacher, as well as his first love. He has experienced ardor for the fish; now he knows it for the insects, for he has made the connection between them and he discerns a chain of life that is critical to his enjoyment and to his commitment. The river has taken possession of him; the ardor he has had for fish now includes the river itself. He becomes its voyeur, then its companion, and finally its champion, its defender. He will fight to preserve its fish, its beauty, and most importantly its health. It has become *his* river, a member of his family and more. Elder fly fishers are the earth's true river ecologists, for they know how much there is to lose, and how it is lost.

A FLY FISHER'S LIFE LIST

I must tell my grandson, Ben, about the great fishes that lie ahead for him—and how the elders admire them. I will explain it like this:

First there are the brookies. The elders know that these "natives" have retreated to the highlands to make their last stand. They are aware that this native fish of the Northeast has been moved aside in the lowland streams by the newcomers, the leaping rainbows from the West, and the somber, selective browns from Europe. They also know that acid rains and snows have poisoned the tiny highland waters, killing the habitat where the brookies slowly dwindle in numbers. They know that the brookie has invaded the waters of the Rockies, where, with the brown trout and rainbows, it displaces the Trout of the Shining Mountains, the cutthroats.

The elders know the Atlantic salmon, *salar* the leaper, and how it rises to take the dry on long slicks where it can be skated on a riffling hitch. They know of *Salmo salar's* rapid decline across the North Atlantic, and the many causes that have led to its struggle to survive where man has intruded. They know about steelhead and how the fish, like Atlantic salmon, are born in freshwater streams, where they grow into smolts and then run to the sea and return as adults. In the winter they lie deep in the pools and runs and the fly must be presented there to catch them. In the spring they spawn in the headwaters and in the summer they will take flies skated over their heads. They leap like Atlantic salmon, and like salmon, they are the fly fisher's ultimate fantasy, the stuff of dreams. They are disappearing now, Ben, as man fulfills his industrial dreams.

The elders have, in their lifetimes, observed the decline of the rivers with industrial and domestic pollution and the disappearance of fish that followed. They have also witnessed the river cleanups and the revival of some fishes and the hatches that feed them. They have seen the smallmouth and largemouth bass repopulate rivers that once caught fire. The elders have returned to those rivers with their fly rods to match the mayfly hatches where now thousands of smallmouth rise each evening. They have returned to the rivers with their hair bugs and their modern epoxy patterns to fish for largemouth, too.

The elders know that you can teach an old dog new tricks. They have taken to the shorelines where the striped bass have returned after three decades of decline due to excessive fishing. Like children with new toys, the veteran fly fishers pursue schoolies and take and release them by the dozen. They stalk the saltwater flats and sight fish to larger mature stripers that prowl the saltwater margins from Long Island to Cape Cod. They haunt the jetties during foul weather for forty-inch fish; they patrol the Chesapeake Tunnel waters during November for fifty-inchers. They chase the stripers as they move southward in autumn from Nova Scotia to Martha's Vineyard, and to Oregon Inlet in the Outer Banks. They fish the bluefish blitzes along the shorelines of New Jersey and meet the false albacore and bonito from Rhode Island south to Point Lookout, North Carolina.

They prowl the spartina grass flats for red drum in Pamlico Sound and along the sheltered flats behind the barrier islands and in the rivers from North Carolina to Georgia, Cape Kennedy, along the western shorelines of Florida and across the Gulf Coast to the Padre Island flats.

This is a movable feast, this chasing of the fly fisher's life list. It takes him far afield, to the Pacific Ocean structures in search of pelagic billfish that light up like shimmering blue neon signs when they chase bait to kill and eat. No one can describe that first sight of a bill appearing behind a teaser and the flashing of an excited sailfish or marlin about to pounce. The captain throws the boat out of gear and the mate yanks the teasers back and tosses the frustrated fish a bundle of feathers as large as a sparrow and as bright as a macaw. He engulfs it and turns sideways, showing his entire seven-foot length in full electric display.

When struck, the fish leaps and leaps again and then greyhounds away across pacific blue waters, almost to the horizon.

On the Pacific the veteran discovers rooster fish, sixty-pounders seen backlit in sixteen-foot waves as they patrol the breakers near Cabo. He learns that they are smell and sight hunters that must be chummed with live bait to propel them to Tenth Level predation so they will take a fly. He discovers dorado at sunrise, fishing from *pangas* with Mexican guides who toss live sardines to the greyhounding predators to excite their killer instinct until they take any fly you throw. At night he lies in bed listening to blue whales singing in the darkness. He explores on long-range boats the Pacific banks, where white marlin mix with yellowfin tuna, skipjack, and wahoo that take the fly and leap twenty feet into the air and burn out high-tech reels and break the strongest graphite rods.

The elders have taken the Big Three, and some have done it quickly at Cuba's Jardines de la Reina, the only place where a grand slam is *expected*. They are experienced with bonefish, beginning with the schoolies of the Yucatán Peninsula. But in their sunset years they search for double-digit bones at Andros Island along its northwest shoreline, in Biscayne Bay and on the turtle grass flats of the Florida Keys. Their pursuit is quality, fish that take you into your backing until the spool shows and sweat beads your brow.

Bonefish may become their obsession. They may chase them across the flats of the world, as far away as the Seychelles in the Indian Ocean and Christmas Island or the Solomons in the Pacific. This hunt will teach them the flats and their creatures, but mostly it will teach them love for a fish that hides itself by reflecting the bottom off mirrorlike scales and dashes two hundred feet at twenty-five miles per hour when hooked. Its natural history will enthrall him in his expanding universe of fish and knowledge.

The elders have stood their watches, staked out along Buchannon or some other bank waiting for shots at passing tarpon. They have changed their behavior: They no longer keep banker's hours at the dock. Now they depart before daylight and fish the channels around Key West and as far north as Islamorada before the jetboats flame the flats and drive the fish away. Now they fish in the evening darkness, jumping tarpon along the bridges at Vaca, Bahía Honda, Seven Mile, and other cuts. Today the veterans fish laid-up tarpon, where happy fish relax while awaiting a change in the tide to resume their feeding and their travels. Now the veterans fish the recently discovered "worm hatch" in May when the emergence of the saltwater worm sets the table for a tarpon feeding frenzy. The ancient tarpon remains the most explosive and acrobatic of all fly-rod fish, and the ultimate rush comes to the fly fisher when it chases the fly and inhales it in gin-clear water ten feet from the boat.

Permit are the holy grail. Saltwater fly fishers feel existentially diminished if they have not taken one, and they admit to failure only when flushed from cover. They should not blush: Permit are occasionally seen on the bonefish flats of the world, but they are shy creatures that seldom take a fly no matter how well it is tied and presented. If the fish are not feeding, there is no way to entice them to the fly, except with chum tossed overboard near a wreck or along an outside-flat travel channel. Del Brown, the anointed king of permit on a fly with more than four hundred taken, has taught us how to catch them fairly on the flats. The best places to succeed include the Marquesas Cays off Key West, and on the flats of Cuba, Belize, and the Yucatán Peninsula, from Boca Paila south to Ascension Bay.

My enduring memory is of three fifty-pounders drifting down a flat at Chubb Cay in the Bahamas. One tipped on my Merkin for a look, but they continued on their way. The woulda, coulda, shouldas have persisted in my dreams.

The Pacific salmon get little respect from fly fishers. Perhaps this contempt was born a century ago, when the rivers from the Northwest to Alaska were seasonally packed with salmon, which were slaughtered for food. Only recently have the bright fish gained the luster of a prize catch; now we have learned how to catch them on a fly thanks to the efforts of Jim Teeny and the lines and fishing techniques he created. All fly fishers should include king, silver, chum, and sockeye salmon on their life lists.

Kings enter Alaska's rivers early in summer and continue in some rivers as far south as California as late as November, with some returning in spring. They are the most powerful anadromous fish for their size to enter fresh water to spawn, and when they are in a taking mood, they eat a fly as hard as any fish and run as far and jump as high as Atlantic salmon. A bright fifty-pound king salmon is virtually impossible to stop, and it fights with an unsettling intelligence.

Chum salmon get no respect either, perhaps because they were dried for dog food by Native Americans and early settlers. But when they are fresh and the downriver pools are full of them, the sight fishing to vast schools that ripple the surface can be the equivalent of Alaska bonefishing, with a hookup and a thrashing fight on every cast. There is no better way to teach a beginner the joy of catching fish than with fresh-run chums fished on a pink Polliwog swung slowly on a tight line down current to a pod of chums newly arrived in the river.

Silvers are closely related to rainbow trout, which they resemble in shape and fighting behavior. I love them for their willingness to take a fly on the surface, and for their aerial acrobatics. They arrive when the season is long in the tooth and a bitter sweetness hangs on the air and the bears feel an urgency to eat in preparation for denning. The rivers are charged with fish and bears on missions and the silvers rush up from the sea and bump around your legs in an irrepressible charge to spawn, to perpetuate their genes and die. They provide us with fifty-fish days as the autumn solstice approaches, when the northern lights dance and the bears pad the banks and charge crazily across the shallows.

Sockeyes come late, and take the fly poorly. They swim with their mouths open, which has induced some guides to "line" them, guiding the line into their mouths and pulling it into the outside of their jaw. This is unfortunate because bright sockeyes can be caught with careful nymphing techniques and small flies. In the late-evening half-light they begin their massive movements upstream, swimming through riffles no more than four inches deep. Then they gently mouth a small dead-drifted wet fly, and fair hookups result in spectacular acrobatics. A fresh twelve-pound sockeye runs, leaps, and tears up the river, racing through shallows deep into your backing. They are the after-hours finger candy of the Alaska rivers, and they are largely ignored except by the bears.

I began my fishing with chars—the brookies—graduated to the Dolly Varden, then the kungia of Kamchatka, and finally the Arctic char. The Dollies, sea run and landlocked, get slight mention, because they are easy to catch and small due to overfishing by commercial and subsistence fishers. They play second fiddle to the rainbows, the salmon, and the ubiquitous and easy grayling, which charm the light-rod dry-fly fishers between innings on the Alaska rivers.

But Dollies are so, well, *charlike*—brilliantly colored and without scales, and so eager to take a fly—that we care not that they seldom take us into our backing or fail to leap. We look upon them as children of that mysterious interface between the sea and the land, commuting out and in to feed and to spawn. And whether they are the Arctic chars, flamed for spawning, or the landlocked strains, we cherish them for their bullish fights and their coats of many colors. A day catching char is like a holiday at the beach—all cotton candy, ease, and carefree relaxation.

Inconnu means "unknown" in French. They make the fly fisher's life list because they look like herring, freshwater tarpon perhaps, and they leap acrobatically in fifty-degree water. They are not of the herring family. They are a side dish, worth fishing in Alaska (the Kobuk River) or in the Yukon Territory for their acrobatic fights.

Ouananiche is the beautiful Native American word that describes the landlocked version of the Atlantic salmon. No fish is more delicately appointed in coloration or more aristocratic in behavior. I think of ouananiche as aquatic dancers, like the flying fish of the Caribbean Sea. I have trolled for them in the old way along the shorelines and inlets of Lake George. The flies were well-dressed streamers—Montreal, Governor Aiken, Nine

Three, and Parmachene Belle—that were tied by the long-gone streamer fishermen who haunted the lake districts of Maine, New Hampshire, and the Northcast Kingdom of Vermont.

We fast-trolled for them at ice-out and the salmon always seemed to take the fly as the boat swung and the fly hesitated slightly, dipped, and then the line tightened. It paid to make the swing at the brook inlets, where the smelt were running to spawn. You trolled those places with special anticipation and made the swing there knowing it was your best chance.

Nothing compares to the take of a ouananiche on a tight line. Your arm jolts and the cold lake spits forth a shiny eight-pounder. It leaps and leaps again and you wish it would never stop. In the net it shines like polished nickel.

I have also hooked the ouananiche on a long line on Labrador lake outflows where the baitfish gather and the lake trout and landlocks prowl for food in the brief sub-Arctic summer. You can catch the ouananiche there on a dry—a well-dressed Size 12 White Wulff greased and cast long to the flow and skated on its tips. You know what will come, so you fish with your heart in your mouth.

The take is exhilarating, like a small depth charge exploding on the surface. You have waited a long time, far away, for that jolt in your arm and the dancing fight that follows. I dream of lowery days on Labrador rivers and lakes and the take and dance of ouananiche.

Redfish are funky, shy, and introverted. I like them that way. When they are working slowly up a flat, alone or in a small school, I glance at them sideways so they will think that they are invisible, a thought that they hold dear. When observed, they slowly tighten, *sensing something*. In clear water they spot my line in the air. They sense pressure waves emitted by the bow of my boat or the slap of small waves against it. They ease away slowly as if to say: *Too tight, man. I'm history . . . I'm outa here*. A spooked bonefish smokes the flat; a redfish slinks away.

This is a fish designed to get little respect. They say that its mouth is inferior, like the mouth of a bonefish or a sucker. In fact it is superbly designed to suck highly nutritious foods from the world's richest environments, the bottoms of grass-flats interfaces between the sea and the land.

We were ignorant of this wondrous ecosystem when I was a child. Only the shrimp, clam, crab, oyster, and fin fishermen knew of it and, for four centuries, had it to themselves. This is the nursery of the drums, black and red, and the striped bass and the vast food chains that feed them. Even as the recreation-home developers turn a hungry eye to these wetlands, even as the pig farmers build their vast pork factories and pollute the headwaters, even as the paper makers contend for factory water by the acre-foot along their tributaries, even as commercial fishermen with factory ships overfish their saltwater boundaries, even so, the redfish thrive.

These are not *inferior* fish. They grow to more than fifty pounds, and they require the most sophisticated fish-hunting skills to approach silently when they are in the grass and weeds on incoming, where tides may reach to six feet, where the hunt begins as large schools patrol the open flats, waiting to make their feeding forays into the plants.

Nothing raises my nerve ends more quickly than a school of redfish moving down the flat toward me. They are glimpsed first, almost as an apparition, not entirely perceived or believed. The school is like a moving shadow, an animation within the water. You must believe, for it animates your hunting instincts. Your nerve ends tingle. As a reflex, you begin to feed out line onto the foredeck. The guide whispers "Shhh!"

for he knows that the sound of the reel can be heard for great distances under water.

You fidget . . . waiting.

Then he says "Cast! One backcast!" and you shoot line behind and stroke hard to load the rod down into the butt. You throw eighty feet. The school senses something and changes its angle of approach slightly. The fly lands just short. Somehow the school *knows*, feels a pressure wave from the bow, senses the line in the air . . . something suspicious that it has experienced before.

A fish breaks from the pack and charges the fly. The approaching bow wave is bonefishlike, only larger. When the guide says "He's on it! Stick him!" you lift and tighten reflexively. Then it's away and up the flat. Reel music mixes with the clean fresh smell of the salt flats. A blue heron, disturbed, lifts in slow motion and flies aristocratically away.

Go to the ends of the earth: it's worth the trip. Tierra del Fuego is the nethermost place, as far south as you can go without hitting ice. What you will find there is globally strange, including sea-run brown trout transported there late in the last century by Europeans. These emigrants—there were no salmonids south of the equator—are the largest members of their subspecies, and they are pearls of great price to a world-traveling fly-fishing gentry.

These fly fishers attempt to throw lines where williwaw winds rattle the rooftops in the night. The fish are worth the effort, for they come up from the sea fattened into silver torpedoes that take the fly and bulldog their way into your backing. They are not Atlantic salmon, but they are certainly second best. And they arrive as seasonal visitors in a fabled Darwinian land. He marveled at the camel-like guanaco, and the native Patagons and Tehuelches in Magellan's Land of Fire. He described the Magellan geese, the caracara, and the many other birds, including the Andean condors whose shadows cross the steppes of the cordillera like spirits laying claim to a land that has no boundaries and that diminishes humans into windblown specks on the horizon.

On the Rio Grande a fly fisher tries to de-aerialize his fly line by roll casting an entire line downwind. And when he pees, his trickle becomes a golden mist floating in a cloud around him before drifting away toward Chile or Antarctica. He considers his place in the universe slightly diminished. And later, as the condors ride overhead on a hillside updraft, he hooks something very large and it heads downstream in the direction of the Falklands and he asks himself if anything can be better. Nothing, except perhaps an *asado* (a side of lamb, washed down with Argentine reds and *pisqo* sours) at the lodge.

He can head northward to the Rio Gallegos and its tributary Rio Teniente for river browns and sea runs, and then northward to the Andean foothills of the Argentine Patagonia to fish the big browns, rainbows, and brookies around Esquel. There gauchos wear *bombachas,* holler "Hola!" and drink mate and children are superb horsemen and sheep outnumber humans. He can fish the windswept Rio Chubut for rainbows and browns and expect thirty-fish days on drys drifted along the banks. He can fish the boca of the Rio Futaleufu, then drift it, then drift it farther downstream, below the dam where it becomes the Rio Grande, the closest thing to a giant spring creek that South America offers. The fish there feed in midriver pods and you sight fish to them with downstream reach casts. Or you pound the banks with large black or charteuse Woolly Buggers, Strip Buggers, or Chernobyl Ants dead-drifted close along the bank cover. The river's clear *lagunas* provide some of the world's best sight fishing to large cruising browns and rainbows.

Around Junin de los Andes the rivers that drain the Andean steppe have written the book of Patagonian fly fishing since the 1950s explorations of Joe Brooks and Ernest Schwiebert Jr. The Rio Malleo is South America's best match-the-hatch dry-fly river; the Collon Cura matches the Madison River of the 1970s in quality of boat fishing for large rainbows; the Rio Traful, once the best Sebago-strain landlocked salmon river on the continent, is now partially owned by media mogul Ted Turner, who closes his side of the river to fee fishing.

He can head farther north to the northernmost rivers of Argentina and the southern rivers of Uruguay and fish the freshwater dorado, a fish that has been called the toughest combatant in fresh water, or he can head farther north into Amazonia, where the cichlid peacock bass grow to more than twenty pounds and make bull rushes into bank cover while you clamp your reel and hope.

Most fly fishers know about the bonefish of Christmas Island and their sizzling runs, but few have experienced the four or more species of trevally that roam along edges of the flats there and on such Pacific flats as Bikini Atoll and Midway Island. These fish require 12-weight rods and three hundred yards of backing, and then you'll be lucky if they do not break you when they head for the reef and dive into deep blue water. There are many other species of fish on these Pacific flats that will challenge fly fishers in the decades to come, but they are faraway islands and difficult to reach. They are a rich man's game but worth dreaming.

There are Guinea bass, the most difficult freshwater fish to land. There are flats fish in Australia that will take the fly and run like bonefish. There are saratoga and barramundi and other river fish along the northern coast of Australia, far out there where salt-water crocodiles and aborigines own the land and the water.

That is how I will tell my grandson about the fishes, the ones that he can catch and examine in fulfilling his fly fisher's life list. I will hand the Golden Thread to him. And if I do not catch them all before I rest, perhaps he will continue for me. He will find the trip worth taking. He will find the fly fisher's life full of joy and fulfillment—a gift.

Split the Lark and you'll find the music,
  Bulb after bulb, in silver rolled,
Scantily dealt to the summer morning,
  Saved for your ear when the lutes be old.

Loose the flood, you shall find it patent,
  Gush after gush, reserved for you;
Scarlet experiment! Sceptic Thomas,
Now, do you doubt that your bird was true?

Emily Dickinson
Selected Poems
Copyright 1993
by Random House Value Publishing, Inc.